MILAN

churches, museums and monuments

Texts by
Claudia Converso

Published by KINA ITALIA

KEY	Page.

FIRST PART

1 CASA DEGLI OMENONI Via degli Omenoni — 27
2 HOUSE OF A. MANZONI Via Morone, 1 — 27
3 DUOMO Piazza del Duomo — 8
4 GALLERIA VITTORIO EMANUELE II — 18
between Piazza del Duomo e Piazza della Scala
5 THE LOGGIA IN PIAZZA MERCANTI
PALAZZO DELLA RAGIONE Piazza Mercanti — 26
6 DUOMO MUSEUM, Piazza del Duomo — 14
7 MUSEUM OF MILAN
CIVIC MUSEUM OF CONTEMPORARY HISTORY Via S. Andrea, 6 — 33
8 POLDI PEZZOLI MUSEUM Via Manzoni, 12 — 28
9 THEATRICAL MUSEUM OF LA SCALA Piazza della Scala — 22
10 ARCHBISHOP'S PALACE Piazza Fontana, 2 — 17
11 PALAZZO CLERICI Via Clerici, 5 — 32
12 PALAZZO MARINO Piazza della Scala — 24
13 PALAZZO REALE Piazza Duomo — 16
14 PIAZZA FONTANA — 17
15 SAN FEDELE Piazza San Fedele — 26
16 SAN GOTTARDO IN CORTE Via Pecorari — 17
17 SANTO STEFANO MAGGIORE Piazza Santo Stefano — 26
18 LA SCALA OPERA HOUSE Piazza della Scala — 20

SECOND PART

19 AMBROSIAN LIBRARY AND ART GALLERY Piazza Pio XI, 2 — 36
20 DARSENA - NAVIGLI - PORTA TICINESE Piazza XXIV Maggio — 47
21 SAN CRISTOFORO SUL NAVIGLIO Via San Cristoforo, 1 — 47
22 SAN LORENZO MAGGIORE
COLUMNS OF SAN LORENZO Corso di Porta Ticinese, 39 — 38
23 SANT'ALESSANDRO Piazza Missori — 35
24 SANTA MARIA DEI MIRACOLI BY SAN CELSO Corso Italia, 37 — 46
25 SANTA MARIA BY SAN SATIRO Via Speronari, 3 — 34
26 SANT'EUSTORGIO Piazza Sant'Eustorgio, 1 — 42

THIRD PART

27 CA' GRANDA - FORMERLY MAIN HOSPITAL
(STATE UNIVERSITY) Via Festa del Perdono, 5 — 48
28 PALAZZO CUSANI Via Brera, 15 — 58
29 PALAZZO SERBELLONI Corso Venezia, 16 — 53
30 PALAZZO SORMANI-ANDREANI Corso di Porta Vittoria, 6 — 49
31 PIAZZA CINQUE GIORNATE — 50
32 PIAZZA MISSORI — 48
33 BRERA ART GALLERY Via Brera, 28 — 59
34 ROTONDA DELLA BESANA Via San Barnaba — 49
35 SAN BABILA Piazza San Babila — 52
36 SAN CARLO AL CORSO Corso Matteotti, 14 — 52
37 SAN NAZARO MAGGIORE Piazza San Nazaro — 48
38 SANTA MARIA DELLA PASSIONE Via Conservatorio — 50
39 VIA BAGUTTA — 52
40 VILLA REALE - MODERN ART GALLERY
PAVILION OF CONTEMPORARY ART Via Palestro, 16 — 54

FOURTH PART

41 ABBEY OF CHIARAVALLE Chiaravalle (south-eastern area) — 80
42 ARCO DELLA PACE beginning of Corso Sempione — 69
43 SFORZESCO CASTLE - CASTLE MUSEUM Piazza Castello — 64
44 MUSEUM OF SCIENCE AND TECHNOLOGY Via San Vittore, 21 — 76
45 PALAZZO DELL'ARTE Via Alemagna — 69
46 PALAZZO LITTA Corso Magenta, 24 — 76
47 PIAZZA DELLA REPUBBLICA — 78
48 SAN MAURIZIO AL MONASTERO MAGGIORE Corso Magenta, 15 — 76
49 SANTA MARIA DELLE GRAZIE Piazza Santa Maria delle Grazie, 2 — 70
50 SANT'AMBROGIO - LA PUSTERLA Piazza Sant'Ambrogio, 15 — 74
51 MEAZZA STADIUM - FORMERLY SAN SIRO Via Piccolomini, 5 — 78
52 CENTRAL STATION - PIRELLI SKYSCRAPER Piazza Duca d'Aosta — 79

© KINA ITALIA S.p.A. publication - MILAN
produced and printed: KINA ITALIA S.p.A. - MILAN
sole distributor : F.lli MUZIO - Milan
Photos by: Maurilio Mazzola, F.lli Muzio, Marzari
Making-up: Renzo Matino
All right for texts and photos reserved
Reproduction, even partial, is forbidden

We thank the Ambrosian Library and Cariplo for kindly loaning the photos of pages 36 and 37.

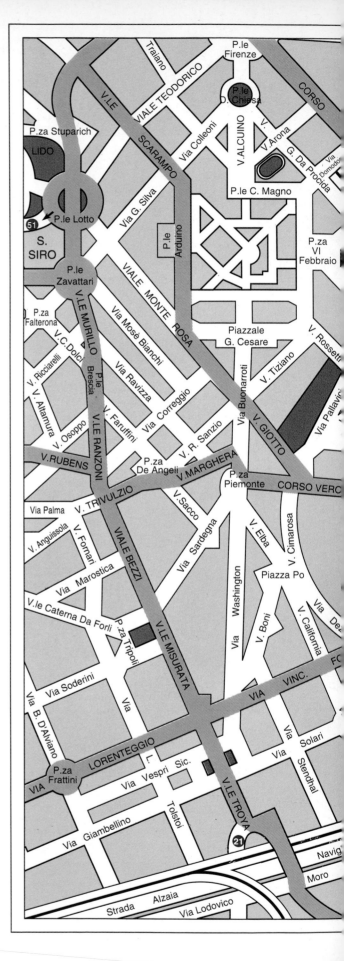

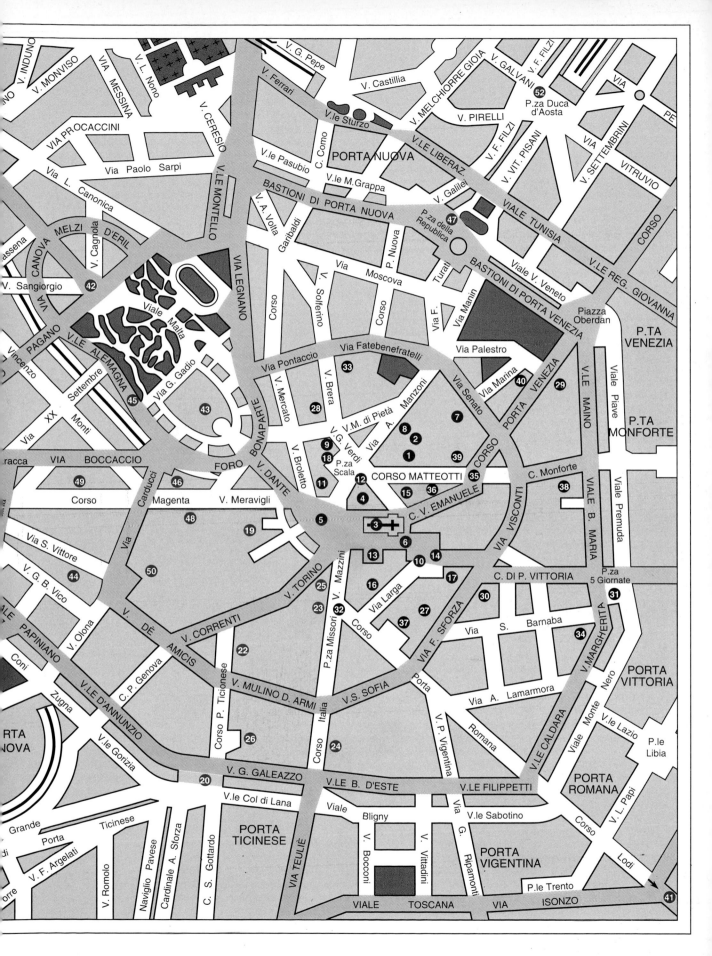

3

INTRODUCTION

The great city of Milan almost always brings to mind a picture of a cold, chaotic city, devoted solely to work, production and investment. This superficial image is so deep-rooted that it is strange at times to think of tourists visiting it. We feel ill-at-ease when imagining them looking at and admiring its treasures surrounded by this bustling and apparently non-stop activity. Nevertheless it only requires broad-mindedness to enter a city and let it show its true face through its streets, monuments, palazzos and churches, and its people, to understand how different and fascinating Milan is. Naturally, unlike many other historical cities in Italy, it is not only a tourist sight, on the contrary it is a melting pot of hundreds of different and (at least apparently) conflicting aspects, which only reveal the combination for unlocking the city gates when taken as a whole. The complex history of Milan alone demonstrates the outstanding features of the city and its population: stubbornness, fond devotion to work, acceptance of new ideas and any potential improvement, even from the outside, willingness to take a critical attitude towards choices and decisions without blindly clinging to the past and tradition when they involve standing still or turning back, ability to cope with even the most difficult situations with great determination and courage. All this can be summed up in a single, blatant characteristic: Milan is alien to and does not tolerate passivity - neither at work, in history, in daily life, in culture and not even in its own art, architecture and town-planning. Inertia is banned from every smallest aspect of its life, in the strong belief that only activity, in whatsoever form it takes, can enrich, not only materially but also intellectually and culturally. This is confirmed not only by its prosperous business sector, the location of the most important stock exchange in Italy, the Trade Fair, university faculties recognised worldwide for their high standards, such as the Università Cattolica del Sacro Cuore and the renowned Bocconi, the ever-present and lively cultural and intellectual scene at all levels, the increasingly cosmopolitan nature of the inhabitants, the urban development, but above all its many art treasures, periodically created, restored, enriched, modified or preserved to increase the city's cultural heritage, at the same time laying the foundations for future developments. In this respect Milan is a city of progress, a progress which however has always been able to respect its background, built by the hard work and intelligence of those who, having arrived first, have enabled the city to look forward. The examples of a distinct and indiscriminate break with the past (devastation of some areas of the city, lack of control on building, excessively radical or hazardous social or cultural schemes) have left a deep mark on the face of the city, which now sees them as a warning to observe its own more genuine tradition. This is also progress to which very often outsiders have made a fundamental contribution, whether from Italy or abroad, always welcomed by Milan as confirmation of its uncommon openness to those who arrive there, bringing their experience, new ideas and new projects. Artists, intellectuals, businessmen or mere workers: Milan offers opportunities for everybody.
The places described here enable many of these aspects of Milan to be appreciated to the full, gradually taking shape as churches, sumptuous palazzos, extremely rich art collections, streets and squares harbouring the memory of the events which have marked the appearance and history of the city. Moving one from place to another to admire all these treasures means sinking into the atmosphere and rhythm of this fascinating city, able to evoke it more plainly than any description, however accurate. In the end a general picture will be obtained of the many-faceted face of the city which the Milanese sum up in the traditional saying: Milan l'è on gran Milan - Milan is a great Milan.

HISTORY

The true origin of the city can be traced back to the early part of the 4th century B.C. and a first settlement of Insubric Gauls. The name of the settlement, later Latinised to Mediolanum, indicated the central position of the site (middle place). From the middle of the 3rd century B.C., the Roman expansion reached the Po valley and in 222 Milan was conquered, together with Como and other towns in the area. The Romanization of the ancient Celtic town was a relatively slow progress, so much so that it only became a "municipium" in 52 B.C., thus achieving self-government status. The importance of Milan grew in the imperial era, as witnessed by the considerable archaeological remains, dating back to the 2nd - 4th centuries, which are gradually coming to light, including through recent excavations (beneath the Biblioteca Ambrosiana (Ambrosian Library) in Piazza Missori). A strategic point for fighting the barbarians from beyond the Alps during the Emperor Hadrian's reign, it received the title of "imperial colony". Between 286 and 402 it was capital of the Roman Empire. In the first half of the 4th century Milan was the second largest and most populated city in the West after Rome and also an important centre of Western Christianity. It was here in 313 that the Emperor Constantine decreed tolerance of the new religion and freedom of religious worship. A major role within this historical context was played by Ambrose, formerly an imperial officer during the era of Valentinian II and bishop of Milan from 374 to 397. During this period a refined and mostly religious art form, particularly architectural, flourished in the city (S. Lorenzo, S. Ambrogio, S. Nazaro, the baptistry of S. Giovanni ad Fontes and other sacred buildings on which the Duomo was later to be built) and religious painting, sculpture and craft. When the empire began to decline, the city lost its importance: in 402 the Emperor Honorius transferred his residence to Ravenna, and Milan, left to the mercy of the barbarian hordes, was sacked and pillaged. On 5 September 569 Alboin, king of the Longobards, entered the city. For most of the nobility and the clergy this meant inevitable exile (almost all to Genoa) to return seventy years later. Only towards the 8th century and, later, at the start of the Carolingian era, did Milan regain a central position in Northern Italy, in spite of the fact that Pavia in 781 had been confirmed capital of the kingdom of Italy. This was mostly due to the authority and influence of the Milanese archbishops who enjoyed, in addition to their high religious standing, considerable political power. One of the most important and influential heads of the Ambrosian church of that time was Ariberto d'Intimiano (1018-1045). Initially a supporter of Corrado II the Salic, whom he proclaimed King of Italy in Milan in 1024 and later supported for imperial coronation two years later in Rome, Ariberto subsequently clashed with the emperor when the latter attempted to intervene in the conflicts within the Milanese feudal system. The reaction of Conrad the Salic was immediate: he laid siege to the city several times between 1037 and 1039, but each time without success. Legend has it that on one of these occasions Ariberto donated to the city army the ensign of Carroccio, which was then to accompany the Milanese in all the wars of the communal era. At the same time, the city was in the throngs of intense domestic social struggles, dominated on the one side by the powerful feudal lords and on the other by the prosperous middle class. Formed for the most part by merchants, artisans and men of law, in 1042 this class organised, under Lanzone, a former notary and personal judge of Archbishop Ariberto, a revolt which forced the nobility to abandon the city. The latter's response was immediate: Milan underwent a long siege which only ended in 1044 when a treaty was drawn up between the opposing sides. Far from ending however, in the years immediately following the conflicts, which had in the meantime also taken on religious connotations, were resumed with the shedding of blood between the high clergy, backed by the nobility, and the people. The latter had in the meanwhile joined together in the Patarini (ragamuffin) movement, urged on by the desire for reform of the Ambrosian church, considered too attached to temporal power. The Patarini maintained their importance up to the death of their leader, Erlembardo, during a battle in 1075. Their influence later declined considerably, also as a result of part of the population (particularly the well-to-do) abandoning the movement, deeming it too radical. In later years government of the city was divided between two main factions: the archbishops and a communal body composed of representatives of the people. It initially acted in the shadow of the archbishop's government (and in fact met in the garden of the archbishop's palace, known as the "brolo" (kitchen garden), from which the term "broletto" is derived to later signify the town-hall), and only became fully autonomous at the start of the 12th century, promoting, among other things, schemes for the territorial expansion of the city in order to increase its political, military and commercial power. In the meantime architecture was flourishing with the predominance of the Romanesque style and the city, surrounded by the Naviglio canal, assumed its concentric shape. Thus in a short space of time Milan became the most important city in Lombardy and the Po valley. The conflict with the Emperor Federico Barbarossa was inevitable when, towards the mid-12th century, he decided to place the municipalities of the area under his control. Milan was besieged first in 1158 and forced to surrender by the imperial troops. It rebelled once again and suffered another siege which lasted as long as seven months, to end in March 1162 with a fresh capitulation and extremely onerous surrender terms. This however was not enough to break the spirit of the Milanese who, also helped by allied towns, formed a new movement to oppose Barbarossa's troops. Thus in 1167 the Lega Lombarda (Lombard League) was formed, presided by the Milanese archbishop, Galdino, whose troops on 29 May 1176 challenged and defeated the imperial army in a decisive battle at Legnano. Merchants and artisans acquired an increasingly important role in the social life of the Commune (in 1233 the Palazzo della Ragione was built, Romanesque symbol of the free city), upholding on numerous occasions a policy of opposition to the city's aristocracy. In later decades however, in a series of mixed fortunes, the aristocracy emerged slowly but steadily, initially together with the municipal institutions and later overriding them, to become established definitively in 1277 with the victory of the party of the nobility led by Archbishop Ottone Visconti. Thus began the dominion of the Viscontis which became fully established in 1294 with legitimisation of the power of Matteo Visconti, successor to Ottone, who obtained from the King of Germany the title of imperial representative to govern Milan and its territories. In a short space of time Milan regained its former role as political and economic centre of the region, even extending its dominion towards the end of the century to Pisa, Perugia and Siena. Thanks to the title of duke, which he had received in 1395, Gian Galeazzo Visconti, head of the state of Milan, distinctly dominated all the other lords of Italy. The Visconti age was also marked by the spread of the Gothic style (in 1386 building of the Duomo began) and the arrival of several artists from Central Italy and the rest of Europe who contributed to creating an independent artistic style of the city which converged in the major works of art of that period. Gian Galeazzo, who died in 1402, was succeeded by Filippo Maria, who had to face the attack by the Republics of Florence and Venice and by the Papal State, concerned by the strong expansion and increasing power of the Milanese duchy. His death in 1447, leaving no heirs and hence no successors, was followed by years dominated by attempts by the Milanese to restore the ancient municipal bodies of the Ambrosian Republic, an attempt which nevertheless soon ended, also due to the intervention of powerful noblemen who aimed at succeeding Visconti. The winning contender was Francesco Sforza, son-in-law of Filippo Maria Visconti, who was recognised Lord of Milan in 1450 and duke in 1454. Thus a period of peace and tranquillity began in Milan. The population grew to over 50-60,000 inhabitants; craft, commerce and agriculture prospered in line with the artistic development of the city (Ca' Granda, reconstruction and extension of the Castello Sforzesco (Sforzesco Castle), S. Satiro, S. Maria della Grazie, S. Maria della Passione) which, already extremely lively during the Visconti era, received a further strong boost from the leading artists and men of culture of that time (including Filarete, Bramante and Leonardo da Vinci). This situation was first upset by the arrival of the French troops sent by King Charles VIII in 1494-1495 and later, in 1499, by an actual invasion by King Louis XII's army which forced Lodovico il Moro to abandon the duchy. In 1513 the French troops were attacked and overcome in Ravenna by the Holy League of Pope Julius II. This allowed the Sforzas to return temporarily to power in Milan in the person of Massimiliano, son of Lodovico il Moro. A mere two years later however, the French launched a fresh attack and defeated the Milanese troops in the battle of Melegnano, thus reclaiming the duchy. These events were followed by five years of clashes and devastations, a feature of the complex political situation in Europe at that time with the opposing French, Hapsburg and Spanish powers. Milan and its domains, deprived of a true autonomous government after the fall of the duchy, represented for each one a tempting objective, also due to their strategic geographical location. In 1521 Milan fell into the hands of the Spanish which allowed the return to power of Francesco II Sforza, another son of Lodovico il Moro, who enjoyed the support of the Emperor Charles V of Hapsburg. After the umpteenth battle with the French, who were defeated at Pavia, the Sforza government was apparently restored by the Spanish. In actual fact Charles V maintained strong control of the city and its property, placing his lieutenants alongside Francesco II to lead the government. When the latter died in 1535, the emperor occupied Milan and the duchy. Thus the period of Spanish domination began which was to last for one hundred and seventy years. Although considerably reducing the political autonomy of the city, the foreign dominion did not totally exclude the Milanese from governing, nevertheless only admitting a small group of members of the nobility and of the most wealthy class in the city, all in all about a hundred families. The town council, who could elect members of government bodies, retained an important role. The members of the senate, the most authoritative state body alongside the governor, included the names of many Milanese. At that time the population increased further to over one hundred thousand inhabitants and the economy, despite the extremely burdensome tax system imposed by the Spanish, managed to flourish for a time. The layout of the city was further modified with the construction of the ramparts ordered by the Spanish governor Ferrante Gonzaga. In the area of religion, the period between the end of the 16th century and the first thirty years of the 17th century are characterised by two important figures whose works left an indelible mark on the history of the city: Charles and Frederick Borromeo. Charles, important spokesman for the Catholic Counter-Reformation and proud enemy of the Spanish government as regards the independence of the Milanese Church, was Archbishop of Milan from 1560 to his death in 1584, and was later made a saint. He was replaced as spiritual leader and example for the Milanese by his cousin Frederick in 1595 until 1631. An eminent cultural and religious figure, depicted by Alessandro Manzoni in his novel "The Betrothed", he founded the Biblioteca Ambrosiana (Ambrosian Library) in 1609, and latter annexed a gallery of paintings which was to form the original nucleus of the modernday Pinacoteca Ambrosiana (Ambrosian Art Gallery), and promoted a number of schemes to support the people during the terrible plague epidemic in 1630. This year marked the start of a gloomy period in the history of Milan in the 17th century. Plague, famine and the arrival of the German armies lead to a sudden decline in the number of inhabitants to around 60-70,000 and a devastating recession which hit the city's economy and also affected agriculture. The change from Spanish to Austrian rule in the years of the war of the Spanish succession occurred in 1706, the year in which Milan was taken by Eugenio di Savoia in the name of the Emperor Joseph I, and the military conquest was ratified in 1714 by the treaty of Rastadt. The first positive effects of the new Hapsburg domination were felt around the middle of the century during the reign of Charles VI and above all of Marie-Therese of Austria (1740-1780). A new and more equitable system of taxation was introduced, a reform of local administration and significant religious reforms were introduced, including abolition of ecclesiastical censorship and of the Inquisition. The city's architecture included a number of new palazzos of the nobility and the neoclassical style appeared, to flourish in all its splendour a few years later. The journal "Il Caffé", published between 1764 and 1766, with contributions from the numerous representatives of the Milanese Enlightenment movement, reflected this spirit of reform dominated by the Enlightenment philosophy together with lively artistic and literary activity. The Austrian rule lasted ninety years and ended on 15 May 1796, the day on which Napoleon Bonaparte's army entered Milan. The entire population of Milan hailed the arrival of the great French general, who represented both the liberator from Austrian domination and bringer of the new ideals of the French Revolution, with great fervour and high hopes. In the summer of 1797 Milan became the capital of the newly-formed Cisalpine Republic. However it soon became clear that the present dominators also allowed minimal government autonomy for the Milanese and that their interest in the city and region was mainly guided by profit. The growing discontent was seized upon by an alliance of Austro-Russian troops which, in the spring of 1799, reconquered Lombardy and Emilia. The Hapsburg restoration was short-lived: at Marengo on 14 June 1800, an Austro-Russian-Piedmontese alliance was defeated by Napoleon, and Milan was once again declared capital of the Cisalpine Republic, renamed first of all the Italian Republic and, from 18 March 1805, the Kingdom of Italy. The Napoleonic government invested considerable efforts in achieving its own aims, which also included modest reforms, creating among other things extensive bureaucracy which provided work for thousands of people. The city, which had given the French a relatively warm welcome after the dreaded return of the Hapsburgs, for a few years prospered in terms of population (which finally started to increase again after years of stagnation), culture and economy, despite the intolerable fiscal pressure exerted by Napoleon's government. It was in fact the crushing burden of taxation by the French which led in 1814 to the sudden downfall of the Napoleonic government and the re-appearance of the Hapsburgs. Taking advantage of the violent disorders which broke out in Milan on 20 April of that year, in which the Finance Minister, Prina, blamed for the French tax policy, met a horrible death, they sent their own troops into the city to re-establish law and order. The Kingdom of Italy having fallen, the Austrians attempted first of all to win over the people by abolishing some secondary taxes and improving the layout of the city and the quality of its services. Soon however they proved that they were once again to cut short any hope of political autonomy, thus further widening the already considerable gap between them and the people. Taxation increased, police control become more ruthless and tyrannical and the highly efficient local administration excessively interfering. Censorship was also imposed, hated by the Milanese who had by then adopted high libertarian ideals. The Hapsburg government thus became increasingly the target for strong hostility which was widespread among the people and was best expressed in the writing and activity, including politics, of men of literature and culture. This hostility led to uprisings, the first of which broke out in 1821 and were brutally suppressed by the Austrians. The Carbonari (activists who met in secret to organise the revolt against the government) and opponents of the calibre of Silvio Pellico, Pietro Maroncelli and Federico Confalonieri were sent to trial, condemned and imprisoned in the terrible Spielberg fortress. Other uprisings in 1833, stirred up by Mazzini's "Youth of Italy", did not achieve tangible results, but were immensely important in preparing the ground and minds of not only a small literary group, but of the whole people, for the great insurrection of 1848, recorded in the history books as the Five Days of Milan, Between 18 and 22 March of that year the inhabitants of Milan rebelled and forced the oppressors to flee. Overwhelmed by victory and freedom, the Milanese were however sharply crushed under the heavy Hapsburg yoke with the return of Radetzky as governor. The city of Milan was however by then ready to free itself once and for all from its dominators, nor were they distracted from this purpose by the ruthlessness with which Radetzky crushed further revolts in February 1853 or by the promises of reforms. Thus sympathy with the Savoy dynasty became widespread and led in 1859 to the annexing with Piedmont, a prelude to the later unification of Italy in 1861. At the dawning of a united Italy, Milan, with some 250,000 inhabitants and a rich economic and cultural history, had all the requisites for becoming one of the most important cities in the country. In the second half of the 19th century it played a leading part in a lively development which involved the city layout and the services. In 1867 the gallery bearing the name of Victor Emmanuel II was inaugurated in his presence. This is a magnificent feat of engineering, which changed the appearance of the city centre definitively. In 1864 the central *railway station was opened in the area of Piazza della Repubblica, and in twenty years the Milanese railway system was connected to that of the main cities in Europe. Milan was the first city in Europe to have a public electric lighting system and the first in Italy to have a department store which was later to become today's "Rinascente". The layout of the city, found to be inadequate for the new social structure, underwent radical alterations (often to the detriment of old buildings which may have deserved greater respect) from the demolition of the Spanish ramparts (remains of which can be seen at Porta Romana), covering-over of the Naviglio and a number of new buildings. This was also the period of major restoration work (not always appropriate) of the most precious monuments of the city, including a number of churches and the Castello Sforzesco (Sforzesco Castle) which was given its presentday appearance. At the beginning of the 'nineties, Milan is an established industrial centre with a population which has almost doubled compared to a few decades earlier, also due to the major phenomenon of immigration which has been a constant, albeit fluctuating, feature throughout this century. This background provided fertile ground for the new socialist ideals expressed in the first Italian Labour Day and in the first major strikes: the new social demands created lively conflict with the political and ruling class which on some occasions led to violent episodes. The first world war years saw the city once again ready to welcome the fervour of Irredentism, a cause to which many Milanese heroically gave up their lives. On 23 March 1919 Benito Mussolini chose Milan to found the militant Fascist groups, thus giving rise to a historical episode which was to end dramatically in Piazzale Loreto in Milan. In the years prior to the second world war (characterised in architectural terms by a number of new buildings celebrating the regime - as in 1926 with today's Central Station and with new radical developments to the city centre, above all Piazza S. Babila) the city continued in its frenetic development, traditionally based on its industrious inhabitants. This trend appeared destined to end when the Depression broke out in 1929, which however only slowed it down. Not even the bombs which in 1943 devasted eighty percent of the city and hundreds of factories (including the historical Pirelli, Breda, Alfa Romeo and Innocenti), causing enormous damage not only to buildings but also to the artistic and cultural heritage, managed to stop the Milanese. They started again from scratch and within a few months restored the vital parts of the city. In the 'fifties Milan was the scene of intensive building and rebuilding thus leading Italy's economic boom, a position which it has maintained up to the present time. Both enlivened and shaken by the student protests and by the increasing awareness of the working masses in the 'seventies, Milan also played a leading role in that gloomy period which went under the name of the "Years of Lead" and which, like many others, witnessed the generosity and courage of its people. The remaining years up to the present time show Milan as a leading city in virtually every area of life in Italy, for better or worse, without, as history has shown, subduing its energy.*

FIRST PART

THE DUOMO (CATHEDRAL)

The religious heart and symbol of the city of Milan, the Duomo, dedicated to the birth of the Virgin Mary, stands on the 19th-century square of the same name which houses the bronze *statue of Victor Emmanuel II on horseback* (Ercole Rosa, 1878). Built in marble in the late Gothic style, its size is spectacular (158 m long and a maximum width of 93 m for a total surface area of over 11,000 square metres). The 17th-century façade is divided into five bays with six buttresses decorated with statues and crowned by spires. The support plinths are decorated with biblical or symbolical reliefs (17th-19th centuries). Above each of the five entrance portals (17th century) is a 17th-century window: the one above the largest portal, with a 1790 balcony, has in turn, like the two adjacent ones, another large 19th century Gothic window above it. The portals are decorated with reliefs created between the 16th and the 17th centuries to drawings by Cerano, while the bronze doors are the work of Italian artists of the 19th and 20th centuries. The sides of the building, built between the 15th and the 18th centuries, are also cadenced by buttresses with spires and tall windows. The part corresponding to the transept has additionally, compared to the rest of the building, two double buttresses with internal staircases. The top is cadenced by sloping rooves

BRIEF HISTORY

Building of the Duomo began in 1386 by order of the Bishop Antonio da Saluzzo and, right from the start, observed (albeit freely) the dictates of the Gothic style of cathedrals in the north. The great source of inspiration behind the choice of this style was probably Gian Galeazzo Visconti (first duke of Milan), who wanted to transform the city into a great capital on a level with those in the north of Europe. This wish was fulfilled on the one hand by the use of marble (foreign to local culture) for the cathedral, and on the other by the contribution, together with Italians, by foreign artists, architects and craftsmen who played a highly significant part in the Milanese artistic development. In 1388, on the site previously occupied by a pagan temple, then by the Basilica Nova (later named St. Tecla) erected in the 4th century by St. Augustine (behind which stood the baptistry of S. Giovanni alle Fonti, remains of which are to be found in the area below the Duomo), and finally by the church of S. Maria Maggiore, the foundations were laid for a building with three naves and work on the perimeter walls began. Building was carried out "from back to front", i.e. starting from the apse, so that the façade was only built in 1682 (until then that of S. Maria Maggiore had been used). In 1391 the layout was changed to five naves and 1392 it was decided to increase the height of the naves, the first demonstration of that freedom of expression of the Gothic style which was to characterise the whole building. In 1393 Giovannino de' Grassi produced a design for the apse windows, which Filippino degli Organi put into effect in the 15th century. The second half of the 15th century marked a period of lively debate on the problems linked to the building of the lantern: on instigation by Gian Galeazzo Maria Sforza, Giovanni Nexenperger (at that time involved in building the cathedral in Strasbourg), Leonardo da Vinci, Bramante and Giovanni Antonio Amadeo intervened. The latter designed the final version of the lantern, which was finally constructed in 1490 by Dolcebuono. In the first half of the 16th century Vincenzo Seregni presented the design for a cathedral façade flanked by two towers, thus starting up a process which involved this part of the building for over two centuries. Seregni's design was abandoned when management of the Duomo "factory" was assigned, by the wishes of the Archbishop Charles Borromeo, to Pellegrino Tibaldi, known as Il Pellegrini, who worked according to the rules of the Counter-Reformation, leaving an indelible mark on the Duomo. After having redesigned the presbytery (consecrated by Borromeo in 1577), he presented a new design for the façade, later partly built by Richini in the 17th century. Between this century and the previous one, further designs were submitted by leading Milanese architects (Bassi, Richino, Tibaldi, Buzzi, Castelli). At the end of the century the design by Buzzi, showing a façade divided into five spans with buttresses and spires, was adopted and, by order of Napoleon, Giuseppe Zanoia started work on completing the façade, finished by Amati in 1813. In 1858 the campanile was demolished and in the early 'nineties the spires were completed. The worksite of the major Gothic building in Italy however was destined never to close: in the 19th century, during the works for completing the façade, and then throughout our century, the Duomo has undergone improvement, restoration, decoration, consolidation and cleaning.

1

1) Detail of the Duomo.
2) The gilded bronze "Madonnina" by Perego.
3) A terrace of the Duomo.
4) Central door of the Duomo, bronze work by Pogliaghi.

amd with an evocative sequence of rampant arches. From the terraces, which provide a splendid view of the city and surrounding plain, the octagonal lantern by Amadeo (15th-16th century) can be admired, surmounted in the 1860's by a spire (108.5 m) on which the gilded statue of the "Madonnina" (small Madonna) by Giuseppe Perego (1774) was later placed. The great polygonal apse (end of the 14th - beginning of the 15th century) is the oldest part of the Duomo: flanked by the two sacresties, it has three large windows whose thin marble ribbing (early 15th century) form a huge rose-window in each ogive. The sides and the apse of the Duomo offer a comprehensive overview of the art of statues from the 14th to the 19th centuries with more than two thousand sculptures and as many as 135 spires (the oldest, the *Carelli spire,* dating back to the early 15th century), mostly by Lombard and other Italian artists, but also by foreign masters.

The interior which, as deemed by Charles Borromeo, reflects the rules of the Counter-Reformation, is in the form of a Latin cross with five naves (the central one is double the width of the others) and comprises a transept with three naves and a presbytery flanked by two rectangular sacresties. The space is divided up by fifty-two gigantic clustered columns most of which are crowned by capitals with niches for statues of saints in turn crowned by pinnacles with statues of prophets. The windows are decorated with polychrome glass windows. The floor in marble and stone, begun in 1585 and only finished in the mid-20th century, is decorated with polychrome inlaid patterns.

The counter-façade is dominated by the main central door (17th-19th centuries) with the

states of St. Ambrose and St. Charles on either side and plaque commemmorating the two consacrations of the Duomo in 1418 and 1577. A narrow staircase leads to the area of the archaeological excavations which brought to light remains of pre-existing churches and paleochristian relics (4th century).

In the left nave, with altars which date back to various periods (16th-19th centuries) and which house notable Italian works of art (including two marble slabs with figures of apostles of the 12th century and the wooden crucifix carried in a procession by St. Charles during the plague in 1576), there is the 16th-century baptistry, originally situated in the central nave and transferred in the 17th century. The font is an antique Roman trough. The glass windows date back to the 16th century, except for those of *"St. Michael the Archangel" and "Stories of St. Ambrose"* (20th century).

The right-hand nave houses sarcophagi and sepulchres of archbishops and benefactors (including the *"Sarcophagus of Marco Carelli",* decorated in 1406 by Jacopino da Tradate)

1) One of the magnificent coloured glass windows (detail).
2) View of Piazza Duomo with the Victor Emmanuel II monument, the entrance to the Galleria and thefaçade of the Duomo.
3) "Scurolo of San Carlo", 17th century.
4) Crypt by P. Pellegrini.
5) "The Virgin of Help", 1400 fresco.
6) Memorial to Gian Giacomo Medici by L. Leoni - "Peace" (detail).
7) Marco Carelli sepulchre by Jacopino da Tradate, 15th century (detail).
8) Treasury of the Duomo - the silver "capsella" for the relics of the apostles from the basilica of S.S. Apostoli and S. Nazaro, 4th cent.

and comprises altars in which important fourth and sixth-century works of art are placed. Most of the glass windows were made in the 15th century by Lombard, Flemish and Rhenish artists.

The transept, decorated with glass windows, altars, statues and works dating back to various periods (15th-19th centuries), houses in the right-hand nave the memorial to Gian Giacomo Medici, known as "*Il Medeghino*" (Leone Leoni, 1560) and in the left-hand one the "*Candelabro Trivulzio*" (early 13th century).

In the middle of the Pellegrini presbytery (second half of the 16th century), raised and surrounded by carved wooden choir-stalls, is the sanctuary. The high altar (13th century), consacrated in 1418, has at its top a 16th-century pavilion crowned by a statue of the "T*riumph of Christ*" beneath which is the tabernacle decorated in relief and supported by four bronze angels. Another tabernacle, at the top of the vault, holds the "*Holy Nail of the Cross*". Beneath the sanctuary we can see the beautiful circular crypt by Pellegrini, which leads to the "*Scurolo di S. Carlo*" (1606), an octagonal chapel which holds the glass urn with the relics of St. Charles.

The great windows in the apse show the major renovation work carried out during the last century.

On each side of the presbytery are the two sacresties: the southern sacresty, with a 14th-century portal, and the northern sacresty, whose portal (1389) represents the first sculpture of the Cathedral. Leading off opposite the portal of the first sacresty is the Treasury of the Duomo, which houses exhibits of immense value, such as the silver "*Capsella*" of the 4th century donated by the Pope to St. Ambrose, ivory objects, gilded and set with precious stones, silver statues and precious tapestries.

THE DUOMO MUSEUM

The Museum houses the works taken from the Duomo to be restored: sculpture and architectural elements, models, tapestries, parts of glass windows and screens, in addition to drawings and documents relating to the Duomo "factory", covering the whole, turbulent history of its building.

A visit to the various rooms demonstrates the development of art in Lombardy, also through the influence of foreign artists (Rhenish, Flemish and Burgundian), until it became independent (only the names of Jacopino da Tradate, Bambaia, Amadeo, Solari and Mantegazza spring to mind).

The most famous works include the 15th-century statues of *Gian Galeazzo Visconti and Galeazzo Maria Sforza*, those of *St. Peter the Apostle* (14th century, attributed to Joacobello delle Masegne) and of *St. Paul the Hermit* (1465, Lombard artist), *the Crucifix of Ariberto* (1040) and *the Passion Altar-Frontal*, 15th-century Flemish tapestry, and the 17th-century one of St. Charles, the drawings by Cerano and the sculpture models of the leading Lombard artists of the 16th-18th centuries, in addition to those of the *Madonnina* by Perego and of the portals of the façade of the Duomo. Also of extreme interest is the large wooden model of the Cathedral, begun in 1519 by Bernardino Zenale and continued up to the 19th century, which over the years has served as an indication of the changes and additions made to the Duomo.

1) Scenes from the Passion, 15th-cent. Flemish tapestry (detail).
2) St. Paul the Hermit, work by a Lombard artist of 1465, inspired by Mantegazza.
3) "Madonna and Child", polychrome wood sculpture of 1392, attributed to Bernardo da Venezia.
4) "Sala delle Colonne".
5) Gian Galeazzo Visconti, work of 1478 attributed to G.A. Amadeo.

1) View from the Duomo with the
campanile of S. Gottardo in Corte.
2) The façade of Palazzo Reale.

PALAZZO REALE (ROYAL PALACE)

An extensive, neoclassical building, with a plain façade divided by Ionic pilaster strips and decorated on the front by an attic, and with two side wings. Originally the palazzo of the Broletto Vecchio, the first seat of the city council, stood on this site. Over the years it underwent a series of alterations and rebuilding works by the Viscontis (1330) and Sforzas (1452). From 1535, the palazzo housed the seat of the Spanish governor. In 1594 the first Milanese civic theatre was set up in one of the courtyards and later rebuilt between the 17th and 18th centuries and finally burnt down in 1776. In 1772 Piermarini renovated the palazzo by eliminating the front facing the Duomo, thus converting the main courtyard into the present Piazzetta Reale. For the work he used the pre-existing walls to a large extent and commissioned renowned Italian and foreign artists to decorate the interiors. The building, further altered and extended, was damaged by bombs in 1943 and was for many years left derelict, so much so that the splendid neoclassical interiors are lost forever. Careful restoration has today enabled, among other things, some rooms to be used for the CIMAC the Civic Museum of Contemporary Art, which holds masterpieces of the 20th century both by Italian and, thanks to recent acquisitions, other European artists.

16

CHURCH OF S. GOTTARDO IN CORTE

The church, built between 1330 and 1336 as a ducal chapel (possibly according to a design by the Cremonese Francesco Pecorari) and commissioned by Azzone Visconti, has a remarkable masonry campanile resting on a stone base: the surface with windows, is broken up by slim stone columns running along the edges and by four interwoven arch patterns which circle the tower. The campanile ends at the upper part with an order of two-light windows and a small balcony with columns beneath the belfry, also with columns, and a pointed cone. The interior, rebuilt in the neoclassical style by Piermarini, has a single nave, which conserves a fresco of the *Crucifixion* of the Giotto school and the memorial to Azzone Visconti, attributed to Giovanni di Balduccio da Pisa.

PALAZZO ARCIVESCOVILE (ARCHBISHOP'S PALACE)

Built around two courtyards, the palace, already in existence during the late Medieval period, was rebuilt after the siege by Barbarossa (1162) and finished in 1174. From then onwards it underwent a number of alterations and extensions which, starting from those of 1342-1354 (Archbishop Giovanni II Visconti) and 1493-1497 (Archbishop Guido Antonio Arcimboldi), of which remains can still be seen, continued up to the 19th century. In 1570 St. Charles instigated the most significant intervention by commissioning Pellegrino Tibaldi to design the courtyard of the Canonica (presbytery) (1604). Giuseppe Piermarini is however responsible for the 18th-century façade looking out onto Piazza Fontana which includes the portal by Pellegrini (16th century). The courtyard of the Archbishop's Palace (17th-19th centuries) leads, via a staircase, to the interiors which house, in the private apartments, the collection of paintings with works by Cerano, Tintoretto, Morazzone, Gentileschi, Spagnoletto, Reni and other 17th and 18th-century artists.

3) The campanile of S. Gottardo in Corte.
4) The portal of the Archbishop's Palace, 16th cent.
5) The fountain by Piermarini, in the centre of Piazza Fontana.

PIAZZA FONTANA

The Piazza, onto which the portal by Pellegrini, the main entrance to the Archbishop's Palace, faces, was set out at the end of the 18th century by Giuseppe Piermarini. It takes its name from the fountain standing there, also designed by Piermarini: with its tiered basins, it is decorated, in the small space between the smaller and larger one below, with mermaids astride dolphins, created in 1782 by Giuseppe Franchi. Originally stylistically similar buildings stood in this area, a very lively location of small businesses, including a long, three-storey 18th-century residence and a chequered building again designed by Giuseppe Piermarini. The southern side of the Piazza is occupied by the building built in 1940 by Giovanni Maggi which later became the head office of the Banca Nazionale dell'Agricoltura, still sadly famous today for the terrible bomb attack which devastated it on 12 December 1969 during a demonstration, causing death and destruction. To the east a road (no longer there), commissioned in 1603 by the Spanish governor Fuentes, ran as a short-cut from the Court palace (the present Palazzo Reale) to the palazzo of the Magistrate. The building, which stands in front of the main entrance to the Archbishop's residence on the other side of the Piazza, was begun in 1578 and ended in the 17th century. It was enlarged in the second half of the 19th century and later restored after the second world war, with the loss of much of its former appearance. The building for centuries was used as the seat of the judiciary of the city: the trials from 1821 to 1824 against the opponents of the Austrian goverment, the Carbonari, were heard there.

GALLERIA VITTORIO EMANUELE II

The gallery, which opens in the northern porticos of Piazza del Duomo, is both one of the most interesting and controversial works of architecture in Milan and a lively meeting place for the Milanese. In the second half of the 19th century the administration of the city decided to link up Piazza del Duomo with the "Corsia del Giardino", the modernday Via Manzoni, on which La Scala stands. The construction of a street with porticos and a glass roof was immediately proposed and which initially, before the unification of Italy, was to be dedicated to the Emperor Franz Joseph. The working design of the structure, submitted by the Bolognese architect Giuseppe Mengoni in 1864, included a plan with a central piazza (the "Octagon") with a dome (39 m in diameter, 47 m in height) and two transverse wings (both 14.5 m wide, 32 m high and 196 and 105 m long) and the use of iron and glass for the structural work.

The works were begun in 1865 by the British company "City of Milan Improvement Company Ltd." and were later continued (1869), following the bankruptcy of the British firm, by the municipal administration of the city.

It was opened as early as 1867, in the presence of the King Victor Emmanuel II, to whom it was dedicated on that occasion, and the majestic building was finished in 1878, with the raising of the triumphal arch which looks out onto Piazza del Duomo, a massive construction which nevertheless blends well with the lighter glass-covered structure of the interior.

For the city of Milan this was an expensive scheme, both in town-planning terms (the layout of the city was radically changed) and in financial terms (in the years between the sixth and eighth decade of the century, together with the redevelopment of Piazza Duomo, the building of the gallery required over 40 percent of the city's municipal budget funds). Milanese symbol of the newly unified Italy, the Gallery aroused different reactions: on the one side there were those who admired its size, its elaborate decorations (frescoes, plasterwork, stucco and marble) and new design, and on the other those who stressed the problems, above all due to the use of delicate materials which required restoration work right from the early years up to the present time (in addition to the repairs needed after the bombing in 1943) or even replacement (such as the mosaics which in 1911 took the place of the ruined frescoes in the lunettes under the dome depicting *Europe, Asia, Africa and America*).

The buildings facing the interior are occupied by shops, bars and restaurants, some with period fittings and furnishings.

1) **The central dome of Galleria Vittorio Emanuele II.**
2) **One of the four lanterns beneath the central dome.**
3) **Entrance to the Galleria from Piazza Duomo.**
4) **View of the interior.**
5) **The Galleria seen from above.**

LA SCALA OPERA HOUSE

La Scala stands in front of Palazzo Marini on the north-west side of the Piazza of the same name. Having been decided in 1776, the year in which a fire destroyed the theatre of the Palazzo Reale, building of the new theatre began on the site where the church of S. Maria della Scala stood, commissioned in 1381 by the wife of Bernabò Visconti, Beatrice Regina della Scala. The works were assigned in 1777 to Giuseppe Piermarini, who designed a building in the neoclassical style with a façade in three sections: the first corresponding to the ground floor, with a three-arched portico and terrace; the second with triangular tympanum windows framed by Corinthian columns; and finally the third with the mezzanine surmounted by the pediment with the relief depicting *"Apollo's Chariot Pursued by the Night"*. In 1830 Alessandro Sanquirico added the two side wings to the building.

The architectural sobriety of the exterior - partly due to the fact that at that time the piazza in front of it, which would have inspired more elaborate forms and decorations, was not yet in existence - contrasts with the richness of the splendid interior.

At the opening of the opera season, the *foyer*, redesigned in 1936 and in a spacious hall in white marble with neoclassical style *décor*, is filled with famous names and an extremely elegant public which give the opera house a sparkling and worldly atmosphere.

The theatre, arranged in a horseshoe shape and with perfect acoustics, has four rows of boxes (the two lower ones with the royal box in the middle) and two galleries (traditionally occupied by the most expert and scholarly opera buffs, extremely severe judges of the artists performing on the stage). The elaborate decorations and gilded stuccoes were retouched, modified and enriched first by Giovanni Perego, at the beginning of the 19th century, and then in 1830 by Sanquirico. The stage framed by huge Corinthian columns, already very large, was extended in 1814 to become one of the largest in Italy.

La Scala was officially inaugurated twice: a first time on 3 August 1778 with the represen-

1) The monument to Leonardo da Vinci by P. Magni.
2) Piazza della Scala seen from Palazzo Marino.
3) Portrait of Giacomo Puccini.
4) Portrait of Richard Wagner.
5) The interior of the theatre during a performance.

tation of the opera *"Europe Recognised"* by Antonio Salieri and a second time on 11 May 1946 with a concert conducted by Arturo Toscanini, celebrating the reconstruction and reopening of La Scala after it was damaged during the war.

Of international renown, La Scala, also the location for prestigious schools of further training and specialisation, has always been the scene of major events, with the most widely acclaimed artists of the world of music and opera. Bellini, Verdi and Puccini, to name just a few of the greatest 19th-century maestros, chose La Scala for the opening nights of some of their best works, and even today a huge number of artists are launched on brilliant careers. The La Scala piazza, constructed between 1858 and 1860 and embellished with two Beltrami buildings, both of which were once headquarters for the Banca Commerciale Italiana, has a monument to Leonardo da Vinci at its centre, created in 1872 by Pietro Magni.

3

4

5

1) Portrait of Giuseppe Verdi, by G. Boldini.
2) "Teatro alla Scala", by A. Inganni.

THEATRICAL MUSEUM OF LA SCALA

The museum, next door to La Scala, was founded in 1911. Its rooms divided into themes, it displays precious objects, documents and souvenirs of the history of theatre in the East and West, with ample space dedicated to Milanese theatre, of which it provides a vast overview, from the first civic theatre built in the 16th century by Giuseppe Meda at the Palazzo Reale up to the Carcano and other main theatres in the city and, naturally, La Scala itself. It also comprises a record library, archives and an extremely well-stocked library (mostly legacies) which holds a considerable number of books on opera and the theatre.

As regards the history of the western theatre, documented mostly by material from the Giulio Sambon collection, which formed the original nucleus of the museum, special attention should be given to the ancient musical instruments housed in the various rooms, a precious reminder of the development of techniques throughout history, the objects belonging to famous figures in the theatrical and musical world such as for example the great conductor Arturo Toscanini and the equally famous singer Enrico Caruso, the busts, portraits and autographs of famous composers and artists (Gioacchino Rossini, Gaetano Donizetti, Eleonora Duse, Adelina Patti and numerous others, both Italian and foreign), original period sketches (such as those for the costumes used for the first night of "Turandot" by Giacomo Puccini), models of scenery, theatrical costumes, masks, puppets, posters and publications about the theatre. Of considerable interest for the history of 19th century music is the Giuseppe Verdi Collection, which includes portraits and busts of the composer, documentary material on his life, original signed manuscripts and personal items. An

entire section illustrates the history of the Graeco-Roman theatre: it consists of interesting musical instruments of that time, theatrical masks and various items (bronzes, vases, statuettes) discovered during archaeological excavations in various sites, including an Italic scyphus of the 3rd century B.C. decorated with scenes from the popular theatre. Finally there are the rooms dedicated to theatre in the East and comic theatre.

An outstanding painting preserved in the Museum, together with the numerous portraits, is the one entitled "*Il Teatro alla Scala*" (1852) by the Brescian painter Angelo Inganni. This work, in which La Scala is shown from the presentday Via Manzoni, offers a precious demonstration of the arrangement of the area in front of the opera house before the piazza was opened.

3) Portrait of Giuseppina Strepponi Verdi, soprano and wife of Giuseppe Verdi.
4) Portrait of Arturo Toscanini, conductor.
5) Portrait of Adelina Patti, soprano.

PALAZZO MARINO

The Palazzo, seat of local government and a masterpiece of 16th-century architecture, was commissioned in 1553 by a rich banker from Genoa, Tomaso Marino, from Galeazzo Alessi. On the latter's death (1572) only the façade of the rectangular-plan building looking out over Piazza S. Fedele was completed, while the other parts were finished (amongst the financial problems of the heirs of Marino and changes in ownership) in later centuries: the decorative grand staircase at the end of the 17th century, the front looking out onto Piazza della Scala as late as 1892 by Luca Beltrami who designed it basing on that of Alessi.

The façade by Alessi (perfect demonstration of the synthesis of styles and decorative and architectural elements which were a feature of the Perugian architect) has three tiered orders: at the Doric ground floor, at the first Ionic floor and at the upper level with pillars and hermes which support the cornice with the balustrade above. All four façades have portals, the two of the main fronts have a balcony supported by coupled Tuscan columns. In the interior we can find the grand courtyard, with the beautiful open gallery resting on coupled columns with fully curved arches and decorated with lion and female hermes and a large number of friezes both on the pillars which are spaced along the parapet and on the cornice.

1) The entrance portal.
2) The inner courtyard.
3) View of the façade.

BASILICA OF SANTA MARIA DELLA SCALA BY S. FEDELE

Symbol of the Counter-Reformation, the church was begun in 1569 on a design by Pellegrini and completed in 1835. Worthy of note on the outside are the two-order façade and the left side with its Corinthian columns with windows and niches. The interior, with a single nave, has 16th-century paintings and precious wooden confessionals, also from the 16th century.

BASILICA OF S. STEFANO MAGGIORE (OR IN BROLO)

The church, originating in the 5th century, was destroyed by fire in 1075, rebuilt in the 12th century and then constantly redesigned up to the 19th century. Only a clustered pillar of the ancient Romanesque building remains in front of the imposing campanile (rebuilt in 1643 after the previous one collapsed). The three-nave interior shows the neoclassical works.

PIAZZA DEI MERCANTI AND PALAZZO DELLA RAGIONE

This small piazza, begun in 1228, was the setting in the Middle Ages of all the main communal bodies as well as a large number of banks, set up under the open galleries by the merchants of the city. Originally it was a closed square with entrance through six gates which bore the name of corresponding districts of the city. The most important civil Romanesque building in Milan stands there: the Palazzo della Ragione (so-called because it housed the judges who reasoned over court cases), built in 1233 by the podesta Oldrado da Tresseno. The building, with a rectangular plan, has a majestic portico at ground level with two naves supported by giant stone pillars. A niche in the main façade contains a high relief attributed to Benedetto Antelami.

1) Detail of the façade of S. Fedele.
2) The façade of S. Fedele with the monument to Alessandro Manzoni.
3) The façade and the campanile of S. Stefano.

4) Detail of the façade of the Casa degli Omenoni with the telamons scuptured by A. Abbondio, commissioned by Philip II of Spain.

5) The House of Alessandro Manzoni, where the writer lived from 1814 to his death (22 May 1873). It now houses the National Manzonian Study Centre.

6) The Loggia in Piazza Mercanti.

1) "Imago Pietatis" by G. Bellini.
2) "Madonna Enthroned with the Child and Two Angels" by A. Vivarini and G. D'Alemagna.
3) "Trust in God" by L. Bartolini.
4) The entrance staircase of the museum.

POLDI PEZZOLI MUSEUM

Situated in Via Manzoni, this prestigious museum is housed in a fine 17th-century palazzo which was restored in the 18th century and then further altered in the mid-19th century to contain the residence-museum of the nobleman Gian Giacomo Poldi Pezzoli. The museum, which mostly contains works acquired directly by this gentleman or, after his death and thanks to the funds allocated by him for this purpose, by his advisor Giuseppe Bertini, was then further endowed with precious exhibits thanks to donations or contributions from public or private bodies or individual collectors, who in this way aimed to continue the work of the great collector.

Born in 1823, Gian Giacomo Poldi Pezzoli initially devoted his time to collecting weapons (splendid examples of which, dating back to various periods and of different origins can be admired in the museum). Later, encouraged by his mother, he extended the range of his research and interest as a collector and began to take up art. Although advised and guided by experts, the nobleman created a heterogeneous collection, as demonstrated by the presence in the museum of excellent works of art (above all paintings of enormous value or even priceless, such as the famous "*Portrait of a Woman*" by Antonio Pollaiolo which has become the symbol of the museum) next to exhibits, albeit very valuable, of craftsmenship and minor arts (fabrics, rugs, porcelain, Graeco-Roman archaeological findings, jewellery, glass, books, items of furniture). As was customary at that time, Gian Giacomo Poldi Pezzoli wanted to keep all the collected works in the same rooms in which he lived, in this respect taking his inspiration from the idea that it was not so much the works of art which had to decorate the rooms, but instead the rooms had to be adapted to the contents to

MAIN WORKS

The rooms of the museum are organised in themes. The Armeria (Armoury) displays over one hundred ancient weapons collected by Poldi Pezzoli. The Sala dell'Affresco (Fresco room) (which takes its name from the 18th-century fresco by Carloni which decorates its vault) houses precious fabrics including two 15th-century altar-facings. The Sala

28

underline and show off further their beauty and value. For this purpose he had rooms of his own palazzo furnished and decorated adequately, such as the armoury, the bedroom, the Sala Nera (Black room) (the name derives from the ebony panelling with inlaid ivory which covered the walls, sadly destroyed during the second world war), the famous Dante room (by Giuseppe Bertini and Luigi Scrosati), the large entrance staircase and the Salone Dorato (gilded salon) (also known as the Pollaiolo), designed by himself.

On his death in 1879, the nobleman donated the residence and its precious contents to the city of Milan, which thus came into possession of one of the richest and most refined private museums in the world. Nevertheless, as mentioned previously, the generosity of Poldi Pezzoli did not stop there: he in fact set aside a large sum of money in his will as a reserve to pay for maintenance of the works already acquired and for further acquisitions to be added to the museum. In later years, after a period of relative calm, the Poldi Pezzoli museum experienced considerable difficulties, partly due to the financial situation (later

dell'Archaeologia (Archaeology room) houses Graeco-Roman finds (7th century B.C. - 2nd century A.D.). At the first floor, linked to the ground floor by the 18th-century staircase next to which there is a baroque fountain decorated with bronze cherubs, there are the Sale dei Lombardi e degli Stranieri (Lombard and Foreign artists rooms): the first displays works by 15th and 16th-century Lombard artists ("*Madonna and Child*" by V. Foppa, "*Madonna and Child*" by Boltraffio, "*Madonna and Child and Lamb*" by Cesare da Sesto and works by Bergognone, Zenale, A. Solari, B. Luini, G. Ferrari and Marco d'Oggiono). The second houses paintings by Flemish and German artists from the 15th to the 18th century (Lucas Cranach the Elder, Jan van der Meer, Jan Bruegel the Elder) and a large 16th-century tapestry made in Brussels. We then arrive at the Sala degli Stucchi (Stuccoes room) (which conserves part of the original *décor*), with a refined collection of porcelain and statuettes, and the Salone Dorato (Gilded room): in the centre of the floor lies a magnificent Persian rug (mid-16th century) decorated with hunting scenes and interwoven flowers. On the walls we can admire "*Portrait of a Woman*" by A. Pollaiolo, "*S. Nicola da Tolentino*" by Piero della Francesca, "*Madonna and Child*" and "*The Deposition*" by Botticelli, "*Imago Pietatis*" by G. Bellini, "*Madonna and Child*" by Mantegna, and works by Guardi, Cosmé Tura and Vivarini. Works from between the 14th and 19th centuries (Bergognone, Pinturicchio, Spagna and others) are housed in the Visconti Venosta room. In the Sala degli Orologi (Clock room), precision timepieces from the 16th to the 19th centuries including precious sundials and table clocks. This is followed by the Sala del Ghislandi (Ghislandi room) (portraits by V. Ghislandi), the Sala Nera (Black room) (precious furnishings and paintings in addition to the famous sculpture by L. Bartolini "*Trust in God*", 1835), the Sala dei Vetri di Murano (the Murano glass room), the fine Sala Dantesca (Dante room) (frescoes and glass windows with scenes from the "*Divine Comedy*"), the Sala di Palma il Vecchio (Palma di Vecchio room) ("*Portrait of a Courtesan*"), those of Italian artists of the 16th and 17th centuries (Magnasco, Spagnoletto) and bronzes (mostly Renaissance) and those of the gold pieces (jewellery, precious stones, crystals). In the Sala del Settecento Veneto (18th-Century Venetian Room) works by Guardi, Canaletto, Tiepolo, Zuccarelli and the "*Portrait of a Gentleman*" by Rosalba Carriera are on display. The last two rooms hold 15th and 16th century paintings ("*Wedding of Bacchus and Ariadne*" by Cima da Conegliano, "*Pietà*" by Filippo Lippi, "*Samson and Delilah*" by F. Morone. "*S. Maurelio*" by Cosmè Tura, and works by G. Bellini, Mantegna and Lotto).

overcome), but above all to the war: the first world war forced the museum to close temporarily, while the second brought much more serious consequences. During the bombing in 1943 in fact, the Poldi Pezzoli palazzo suffered inestimable damage both to the structure and, particularly seriously, to the furnishings, many of which were lost forever. Fortunately the works in the collection had been transferred to places less exposed to the raging of the war and could thus be returned to their places when, in 1951, the restoration and actual rebuilding work of the building and rooms had finished.

1) Table clock - East German or Polish, 17th cent.
2) "Madonna and Child" by A. Mantegna.
3) Set with cameoes - Italian, 19th cent.
4) "Portrait of a Woman" by A. Pollaiolo.

PALAZZO CLERICI

This building, one of the finest rococo private residences in Milan, was commissioned by the nobleman Giorgio Clerici in the early 18th century as an extension to a previous 17th century building. On the death of Clerici it fell into the hands of the Austrian government and then, from 1813, housed the Appeal Court. The exterior, with a central wing (considerably further back from the road to allow the large carriages of that time to pass through) and two side wings, is decorated with windows set off by fine cornices. The portal in the centre of the façade leads to a large inner courtyard onto which a double-column portico faces. On the right, the grand staircase with three flights, characteristic due to the female figures at the joints in the balustrade, leads to the first floor, where the magnificent rooms of the palazzo are situated. To decorate these rooms Giorgio Clerici commissioned the leading artists of that age, who decorated the walls and ceilings with precious frescoes and stuccoes. The numerous rooms are dominated by the one decorated by Giambattista Tiepolo, who embellished the vault of the gallery with the fresco *"The Sun Chariot Surrounded by the Planets"*. This work, dating back to 1740, depicts against a bright blue sky the chariot of the Sun, a source of light, driven by Mercury and flanked by Venus, Saturn, Mars and a number of other heavenly and sea gods and by the continents. The walls of the room, with their stuccoes and gilded mirrors, are decorated with precious 17th-century Flemish tapestries.

1) **The Tiepolo Room.**
2) **The Tiepolo Room - detail of the ceiling.**
3) **The façade of the palazzo.**

MUSEUM OF MILAN - CIVIC MUSEUM OF CONTEMPORARY HISTORY

The "Museo di Milano" is housed in the Palazzo Morando Attendolo Bolognini, an 18th-century building with a rococo façade, partly altered in the 19th century. It was founded in 1935 on the basis of the Beretta collection to witness the historical, cultural and architectural events in the city. There are displays of works of art, 18th-century furnishings, documents and prints which, as a whole, do not form particularly valuable collections, but nevertheless of considerable historical interest. Particularly worthy of note are the paintings and prints which depict the city throughout its development and in the various aspects of its daily life (such as those which represent the traditional holidays under Spanish and Austrian rule and those of the Napoleonic era) from the 16th to the 20th century. Outstanding among the many artists (Migliara, Durini, Campi, Carcano and others) are the names of Giuseppe Bossi, who painted a number of portraits of Milanese figures (including Parini, Cesare Beccaria and Carlo Porta), Giuseppe Canella, author of *"Corsia dei Servi"* and Angelo Inganni, with his *"View of Piazza del Duomo"* of 1883. The rooms also exhibit posters of plays and original shop signs.

The same palazzo also houses the Civic Museum of Contemporary History: inaugurated in 1963, it preserves important documents, period artwork, arms and various curios relating to the period between the two world wars (1915-1943).

1) "Piazza del Duomo" by A. Inganni.
2) The courtyard of the museum.

SECOND PART

BASILICA OF S. MARIA BY S. SATIRO

A jewel by Bramante, the exterior of the church has two façades (the main one begun in the 15th century and finished in the 19th century, the rear one by Bramantino), a central wing which projects slightly at the level of the false apse, a circular side wing (corresponding to the external wing of the Pietà chapel) with four pediments, the lantern and the Romanesque campanile circled by arched cornices with embrasures and small windows. Part of the interior, with its three naves defined by arches which join at the transept, behind the main altar (with a 13th-century fresco) is the famous false apse by Bramante, a blind wall which, with its reliefs, creates a perfect perspective illusion. The pendentives of the cupola contain figures by Evangelisti (15th century). Situated at the end of the left transept is the Pietà chapel, with 12th-century and older frescoes and capitals of the columns dating from between the Paleochristian age and the 14th century. The *Pietà,* a group in terracotta by de' Fondutis (1483) stands on the altar. The baptistry, or sacresty, in a chapel in the right nave, with an octagonal plan and decorated with niches and pilaster strips, was designed by Bramante.

CHURCH OF S. ALESSANDRO

A perfect example of the baroque style, the church was built at the start of the 17th century as an extension of the nearby college of the Barnabites. The majestic façade, with wide steps in front and two bell towers at the side, has two orders, the upper one (in the rococo style) lower to set off the majestic cupola above the central wing. The Greek cross interior shows the full splendour and richness of 17th-century Milanese art: elaborate pictorial decorations, including by Procaccini and Crespi, decorate ceilings and walls ("*The Life of S. Alessandro*", "*Glory of the Saints*" on the cupola supported by sturdy pillars and columns, "*Virtue of the Saints*"), precious altars (especially the main one) set with hard stones like some of the confessionals along the walls and the pulpit in the central nave, and then the marble, wooden fittings and statues decorating the church throughout.

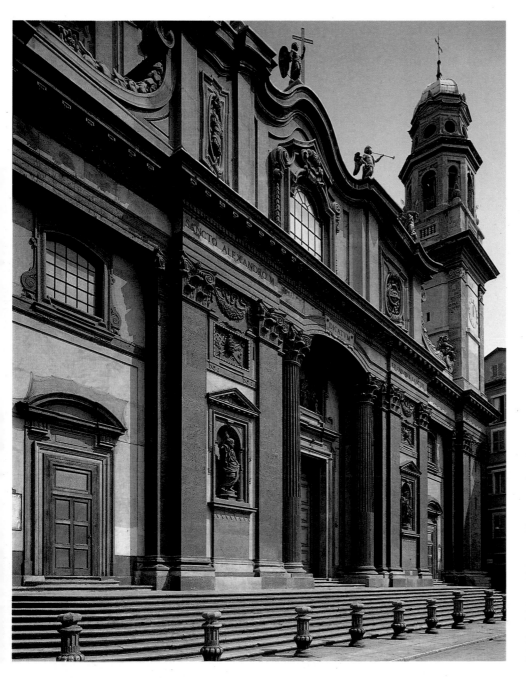

BRIEF HISTORY

The church, built on the site of a previous church which probably dated back to the 9th century, was commissioned by the Barnabite father, Lorenzo Binago, who also designed it. Building work began in 1601 and, around 1629, were taken over by Francesco Maria Richini, and on his death in 1658 by his son Celso Bernardino and then Girolamo Quadrio and Francesco Castelli. As in many churches of the previous century, in which the architects were called upon, in accordance with the rules of the Counter-Reformation, to highlight the central role of the Eucharist in the holy building, Father Binago designed a Greek-cross church in which emphasis was placed on the presbytery. The latter, further extended compared to the original design, was begun by Richini in the second half of the century. The story behind the cupola is interesting: Binago designed it as being supported by isolated columns without worrying about any static problems, which in fact came to light in 1627 when the part already built had to be demolished to avoid collapse. The final structure, lower than the previous one, was finished in the 'nineties by Quadrio. On the exterior, the upper order of the façade, also lower than the lower order, was finished in the first half of the 18th century. A large number of artists and craftsmen contributed to the decoration of the church.

AMBROSIAN LIBRARY AND ART GALLERY

This prestigious institution, housed in the Palazzo dell'Ambrosiana, begun in 1603, was commissioned by Frederick Borromeo. Fully aware of the profound inherent value of the arts, he devoted his time to collecting manuscripts, printed and handwritten texts (including the *"Ilias Picta"*, a priceless 5th-century Graeco-Byzantine work, considered the oldest illuminated book in the world) which were then collected in the so-called Federiciana room, inaugurated in 1609. A first extension was made to the building in 1611, when Borromeo combined the library (the first in Europe to be opened to the public) with a gallery of paintings, the original nucleus of the future Pinacoteca, to which he donated his own works, mostly by artists of the 16th century, the school of Leonardo da Vinci and of that time. The increase in the collections of the library and art gallery did not stop when Frederick Borromeo died in 1631, as demonstrated by the acquisition in the 18th century of the very famous *"Codice Atlantico"* by Leonardo. Robbed by the French in the Napoleonic period of some of the main works (only some of which were later returned), the building was further extended in the 19th century (transfer of the art gallery to the first floor and construction of the present main façade) and then again in 1923 (creation of the reading room, previously a courtyard). Seriously damaged by bombing in 1943, the Biblioteca and Pinacoteca Ambrosiana remained closed until the early 'fifties, when extensive restoration and refurbishment work began. Recent archaeological excavations have revealed important remains (Verona stone floor, 31 B.C. - 14 A.D.) of the huge Roman forum which lay on the site currently occupied by the Palazzo dell'Ambrosiana and adjacent areas.

1) The new corridor leading to the rooms where the ancient texts are to be revealed after restoration.
2) View of the floor of the Roman forum from the time of Julius Caesar, discovered during excavations in 1991, on the right other fragments of the slabs of the Roman floor.

MAIN WORKS

The library holds around 750,000 printed works in addition to 35,000 manuscripts. The main works include: Leonardo's *"Codice Atlantico"*, the "Ilias Picta" of the 5th century, eastern and Arab works and Syriac versions of the Bible, a *"Divine Comedy"* dating back to 1353, a *"Virgil"* by Petrarch illuminated by Simone Martini and a Latin translation on parchment by Giuseppe Flavio.
The most famous work in the gallery is without doubt Caravaggio's *"Basket of Fruit"*, donated in 1618 by Frederick Borromeo to the original gallery of paintings. The various rooms contain foreign and Italian masterpieces of the 15th and 16th centuries (*"Madonna of the Canopy"* by Botticelli, the *Polyptych* by B. Vivarini, *"Madonna and Child Among the Angels and Saints"* by Bergognone, the cartoon by G. Romano for *"The Battle of Constantine"* and the one, the sole survivor of those painted by Raphael for the Vatican rooms, for the *"School of Athens*; *"Adoration of the Magi"* German anon., *"Male Portraits"* by German artists, and works by Brueghel the Elder) with special sections dedicated to Lombard artists and works of the Leonardo da Vinci school (*"Portrait of a Musician"*, by Leonardo himself, *"St. John with the Lamb"* by B. Luini, *"Adoration of the Magi"* and *"St. Matthew at the Stake"* by Bramantino) and to the Venetian painters of the 16th century (*"Adoration of the Magi"*, *"Ecce Homo" and "Mary Magdalen"* by Titian, and *"Portrait of a Horseman"* by G.B. Moroni), works of the 17th and 18th centuries (*"Bishop"* and *"Presentation at the Temple"* by Tiepolo, *"Adoration of the Magi"* by Morazzone, *"Nativity"* by Barocci and *"St. Michael the Archangel"* by Procaccini) and Lombard mannerists of the 17th century (*"St. Ambrose"* by Cerano, *"Madonna with St. Francis and St. Charles"* by D. Crespi).

3

3) "Portrait of a Musician" by Leonardo da Vinci.
4) "Madonna of the Canopy" by Botticelli
5) "Basket of Fruit" by Caravaggio.

4

5

BASILICA OF S. LORENZO MAGGIORE

This church stands near the Porta Ticinese (13th century) and is formed by a central wing with a dome and surrounded by four towers and other smaller features. Next to the original features (a tower, three main chapels, the foundations and part of the load-bearing structure) it has Romanesque parts and those from the 16th to the 19th centuries.

The façade (1894), with a row of Roman columns (1st to 2nd centuries) in front, has a three-arched pronaos with remains of ancient doors on its sides, and two masonry towers, the left side one truncated, at the ends. In the centre of the courtyard stands the bronze copy of the statue of the *Emperor Constantine* kept in the Laterano. The octagonal tambour and the segmented cupola by Bassi rise above the façade. The central plan interior, a spacious octagonal area with four identical two-by-two exedras, is separated by a double order of arches from the peribolos which surrounds it at the lower level and from the women's gallery at the upper level, with a majestic cupola. The main altar faces the entrance, with marble taken from the chapel of St. Aquilinus, a baroque work by Carlo Garavaglia.

1) The "Pusterla" (or smaller gate) of Porta Ticinese, part of the Medieval walls.
2) The façade of the Basilica.
3) The Roman columns of S. Lorenzo.

BRIEF HISTORY

Built between the end of the 4th and the beginning of the 5th century near the imperial palaces, in an area just outside the city walls with other important Roman buildings, such as the circus and amphitheatre, the Basilica was originally, according to some, a Palatine chapel, and according to others an Arian temple which St. Ambrose later converted into a Catholic basilica. The columns in front of the church were almost certainly transported there in the 4th century from another building: the square which separates them from the church was opened in 1935 to replace a portico on which houses stood. The basilica, like the present one, had a central plan, formed by a spacious square wing with exedras, richly decorated with mosaics and surrounded by a peribolos, and on the exterior with a cupola and flanked by four large towers. It was composed of three octagonal-plan buildings: a 4th-century imperial mausoleum (or baptistry, nowadays the chapel of St. Aquilinus), an apsidal chapel (nowadays dedicated to St. Hippolytus) and the 6th-century chapel of St. Sixtus, added by the Bishop Laurence I to bury the bishops of the city. Over the centuries the Basilica was twice rebuilt practically from scratch without however losing its original character. The first time, in the Romanesque period, followed a number of fires and the collapse, in 1103, of large parts of the walls and the cupola. The latter collapsed again in 1573 and this time Martino Bassi supervised rebuilding. His design, drawn up in 1574 and completed in 1619, remained substantially faithful to the pre-existing structure, with some changes to the plan, the interior and a cupola (the largest in the city) with a segmented octagonal shape. In the 17th century two presbyteries were added to the sides of the façade, designed by Aurelio Trezzi as ideal lines joining up with the Roman columns; the sacresty was also built in the 18th century. Finally in 1894 finally Cesare Nava built the façade, altering a previous structure by adding a three-arch pronaos.

1) The cupola of the chapel of S. Aquilinus.
2) The chapel of S. Aquilinus.
3) Interior of the Basilica.

Proceeding to the right in the peribolos we come to the chapel of St. John the Baptist, with a panel depicting the *"Baptism of Jesus"* by Aurelio Luini. From the atrium, with remarkable remains of mosaics from the 4th century, we pass through the Roman portal to the chapel of St. Aquilinus, remained almost unchanged over the centuries. With an octagonal plan and covered by an "umbrella" vault, it has alternating semicircular and rectangular niches above which there is a woman's gallery with traces of ancient frescoes. The niche to the left of the entrance holds the sarcophagus of St. Aquilinus and the one on the right the relics of Galla Placidia, who according to legend was the foundress of the chapel. The semi-domes of the two niches at the back have precious mosaics of the 5th century. In a small square-plan chapel (behind the previous one), with a cupola with frescoes depicting *"Stories of the Refinding of the Body of St. Aquilinus"* a splendid silver urn by Garavaglia contains relics of the saint. From here we descend to an underground level where slabs from an imperial Roman building are housed. Returning to the parabolos we find the elyptical-plan sacresty (1713) and the baptistry. This is followed by the Chapel of the Holy Family, added after 1573. On leaving this chapel we can see two overturned Roman columns in the support pillars of the cupola, one of which still has frescoes from the 13th and 14th centuries. Past the memorial of the Robianis (15th century) we come to the Citizens' Chapel, with a Romanesque apse with traces of 13th-century frescoes and a gothic apse with 15th-century reliefs. The chapel of St. Hippolytus, with a Greek cross interior, is covered by a cupola resting on Roman columns in African marble with Corinthian capitals. The route ends just after the 16th century sepulchre of Giovanni del Conte; the chapel of St. Sixtus, at a lower level in relation to the floor has an octagonal plan and a vault decorated with 17th-century frescoes.

4) **The basilica seen from Piazza della Vetra.**

4

41

1) General view of S. Eustorgio .
2) Exterior of the Basilica.
3) View of the façade.
4) Typical view of S. Eustorgio.
5) Interior of the Basilica, the central nave.

BASILICA OF S. EUSTORGIO

This church was built in the 9th century on the ruins of a basilica built between 315 and 331 by Bishop Eustorgio to contain the remains of the Magi on the site of a 2nd-century Christian cemetery (the only one in Milan, discovered in the subsoil between 1952 and 1966). In 1164 the remains were stolen and taken to Cologne and the basilica was destroyed. A second reconstruction, in the Lombard-Romanesque style, was started in 1190 circa. In the 13th century a number of alterations were made to the interior, from 1297-1309 the campanile was erected and, up to the 15th century, the side chapels were added. Further work, above all to restore the basilica with its original appearance, freeing it from the unsuitable works of the 17th-19th centuries, have been performed up to the 20th century.

The only original features of the façade (1862-1865) are the arched cornice under the slopes of the roof and, on the left, the marble pulpit which in 1597 replaced the previous one in wood. Running along the right side, rebuilt in the 19th century, are the projections of the chapels built between the 13th and the 15th centuries. Past the semicircular apse (9th century), next to the tall campanile, we can see the Portinari chapel (15th century), with the characteristic dice shape and six-sided lantern.

The interior has three naves divided into eight bays with sturdy pillars (with capitals of the 11th and 13th centuries and traces of frescoes of the 13th and 14th centuries) which bear arches on which the cross-vaults rest. The right-hand side chapels can be divided into 15th century ("Brivio", "Torelli" and "Madonna of the Rosary") with frescoes of the 16th and 18th centuries, 14th and 15th century memorials and a remarkable triptych by Bergognone;

1) "Madonna of the Milk", Lombard school, 15th cent.
2) Fresco depicting S. Eustorgio, Lombard artist, 14th cent.
3) Remains of the original cemetery basilica, 4th cent.
4) Marble altar-piece of the main altar, Gothic work of the 14th cent.
5) Arch of S. Pietro Martire by Balduccio da Pisa.

the end of the 13th century ("*Viscontea*", "*S. Vincenzo Ferreri*", "*St. Thomas*" and "*Torriani*"), with frescoes of the 14th, 15th and 16th centuries, 13th century works and admirable Visconti sepulchral memorials (one by Giovanni di Balduccio, 1359) and finally that of the "*Magi*" (second half of the 13th century), with frescoes from the 16th century, and divided into two areas housing, on the right, the sepulchre which contained the relics of the Magi, and on the left a marble triptych decorated with bas-relief (1347). In the presbytery stands the main altar with a marble polyptych from the 14th century. Behind the altar is the pseudocrypt, built in 1537 with 15th-century columns from the cloisters of the convent next door to the basilica. In the centre we can see a section of wall and foundations of an apse possibly belonging to the pre-existing basilica. This is followed by the famous "*Portinari*" chapel (built in 1462 by the Florentine Pigello Portinari to house the remains of St. Peter Martyr), with walls decorated at the top by splendid frescoes by Vincenzo Foppa (1485) and in the centre, on eight pillars symbolising the Virtues, the precious marble sepulchre decorated with bas-reliefs and statues (Giovanni di Balduccio and his assistants, 1338). On the cover of the sarcophagus there is a shrine with three pinnacles with statues of Christ, the Virgin Mary and of saints. A small chapel on the left houses the 17th-century silver urn with the head of St. Peter Martyr. In the chapels of the left nave remains of frescoes of the 13th and 14th centuries and works of the 17th and 18th centuries can be seen.

BASILICA OF S. MARIA DEI MIRACOLI BY S. CELSO

This church was built on the remains of the small one which housed the miraculous painting of the *"Madonna and Child"* commissioned according to legend at the beginning of the 4th century by St. Ambrose to be painted next to the church of S. Celso. Begun in 1490, the works ended a century later with the present complex and stylistically heterogeneous structure to which the leading artists and architects of the time contributed. The richly decorated façade is worth noting, with the huge four-sided portico and the octagonal lantern in front. The three Latin-cross naves (richly decorated with stuccoes, frescoes, statues and paintings from the 15th to the 18th centuries) are defined by arches resting on pillars. The cupola, placed at the junction with the transept and decorated with frescoes, rests on a polygonal tambour. The presbytery, crowned by the splendid choir-stalls and surrounded by the peribolos, also with frescoes, houses the miraculous fresco of the *"Madonna and Child"* behind the precious main altar.

1) **Arch of Porta Ticinese by L. Cagnola.**
2) **The façade of S. Maria dei Miracoli by S. Celso.**

THE DARSENA (BASIN) AND NAVIGLI CANALS

A short distance from the neoclassical atrium of Porta Ticinese, built between 1801 and 1814 by Luigi Cagnola, we find the "Darsena". Also known as the "port of Milan", having served this purpose in the past (the blocks of Candoglia marble arrived here for the Duomo from Lake Maggiore), it was constructed in the early 17th century by the Spanish governor and then extended and altered in 1920. The Naviglio Grande Canal, the largest in Milan (begun in 1777-1779) and the most important for transport and traffic development in Milan, 50 km long and linked up to the Ticino and then with Lake Maggiore, flows into this basin. The Naviglio Pavese Canal however flows from the Darsena, its name deriving from the fact that it joins the Ticino river near the walls around Pavia after having wound its way for approximately 30 km. It was begun at the end of the 14th century as an irrigation canal, although the works were interrupted several times during the centuries and were only finished in 1819.

1) Church of S. Cristoforo sul Naviglio.
2-3) Two characteristic views of the Naviglio Grande.

THE NAVIGLI AREA (Folklore)

The area around the Navigli is the area of Milan where the popular atmosphere and the features of a small community with its own traditions are most apparent, like a village within the city. Along the two Navigli and around the Darsena numerous small crafsmen's shops can still be found: mattress-makers, painters and decorators, bicycle repairers, plumbers, carpenters, potters and glassblowers, surviving without the need to become "arty-crafty" shops as has been the case elsewhere. The Navigli district is also the artists' quarter, with painters' studios on the Naviglio Grande and exhibitions on the bank around the Vicolo dei Lavandai. The first artists arrived here around thirty years ago, possibly attracted by the Bohemian atmosphere and have been arriving ever since. Besides the painters, antique dealers also reflect their precious wares in the dark waters of the canals, either in small shops or on stalls set up every first Sunday of the month with various objects and period furniture. An area like this obviously has its festivities: on the first Sunday in June, to greet the imminent arrival of summer, hundreds of stalls and kiosks are grouped together on the Navigli to display miscellaneous goods and delicacies. Rowing races (several historical rowing clubs have their club houses on the banks of the Naviglio Grande), dancing and singing, and then the fireworks finale celebrated by thousands of people from all over the city and beyond. Great revelry with a folk atmosphere which is partly recreated every Saturday when the areas around the Darsena welcome the "Fiera di Senigallia", a sort of Milanese flea market. Workshops, painters, antique dealers and osterie, which once flourished outside of the city gates, thanks to tax benefits on wine which exonerated it from the dues charged in the city, have remained and launched a tradition of bars, restaurants etc. which nowadays liven up the Navigli area, often to the rhythms of jazz.
There are also significant reminders along the Navigli of far-off times when a number of religious buildings stood there: on the Naviglio Grande the church of S. Cristoforo sul Naviglio, dating back to the 13th century, on the Naviglio Pavese the Chiesa Rossa ("Red Church"), or S. Maria la Rossa, dating as far back as the 9th-10th centuries.

THIRD PART

CA' GRANDA (FORMERLY MAIN HOSPITAL)

Founded in 1458 by Francesco Sforza and Beatrice d'Este as a single hospital for patients living in the city, since 1958 the building has housed the arts faculty of the State University of Milan. The initial design was by Filarete, but building continued until the 19th century with the contribution of the best architects of that time (G. Solari, G.A. Amadeo, F.M. Richini, Pessina and Cerano).

1) Piazza Missori, in the foreground the monument to G. Missori by R. Ripamonti.
2) The façade of Via Festa del Perdono of the State University, by Filarete.
3) The basilica of S. Nazaro Maggiore.

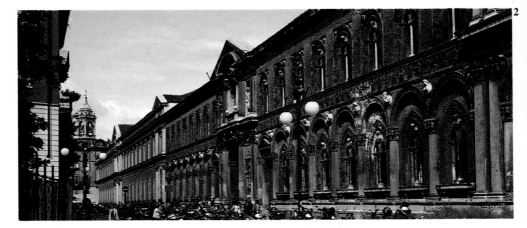

BASILICA OF S. NAZARO MAGGIORE

Founded around 386 by St. Ambrose, it was dedicated ten years later to S. Nazaro when his relics were laid there. Rebuilt on the original structure after a terrible fire in 1075, it was altered and extended in the 17th and 19th centuries and finally radically restored after the bombing in 1943. The basilica, which holds important works of the 15th and 16th centuries, stands behind the Trivulzio chapel, begun in 1512 by Bramantino on commission by the Sforza condottiere Gian Giacomo Trivulzio and never completed.

1) Detail of the church of S. Michele in the centre of the Rotonda.
2) The façade of Palazzo Sormani.
3) Typical view of the internal portico of the Rotonda.

PALAZZO SORMANI-ANDREANI

The palazzo, one of the most elegant 18th-century buildings in Milan, was in fact built in the 17th century, but in 1736 was extended by Francesco Croce to assume its present form. The forward central wing dates back to that year, with its fine ochre façade crowned by the curved tympanum with a balustrade at mid-height which also re-appears in the two convex side wings. The façade facing the English garden is also 18th century (1756). Heavily damaged during the war (the frescoes in the rooms were completely ruined), the palazzo was nevertheless quickly restored in order to house, in 1956, the prestigious Central Library of the city, with hundreds of thousands of books and an extremely well-stocked newspaper and periodical library.

ROTONDA DELLA BESANA

The group of structures (also known as "Foppone dell'Ospedale"), bordered by the fine circular portico, was built around the church of S. Michele ai Nuovi Sepolcri (1713) as the cemetery of the hospital (Ospedale Maggiore), In 1782 the cemetery was closed and it was proposed to transform the building into the Pantheon of the Kingdom of Italy. The plan was however never implemented and the place was used until the 20th century as a hospital for contagious illnesses, laundry and seat of the picture gallery of the Ospedale Maggiore. It is currently used by the city council as an arts centre for art exhibitions and shows.

Around the church of S. Michele (deconsecrated), with its Greek cross shape and fine octagonal lantern which conceals the cupola, runs the magnificent circular wall built by Francesco Raffagno in 1725. Formed by four larger porticoed exedras which alternate with a further four smaller ones with porticos on double columns, the exterior (in brickwork) has arches on pilaster strips.

The buildings stand close to Piazza Cinque Giornate ("Five Days"), in the centre of which stands the imposing monument dedicated to the events of 18-22 March 1848, when the Milanese rebelled against the Austrians, forcing them to flee. Designed by the sculptor Giuseppe Grandi, who completed it in 1895, it consists of an extremely high obelisk and a sculpture group depicting allegorical figures which surround its base. The obelisk (22 m high), resting on a granite plinth, has engraved on its surface the names of those who fell during the uprising (whose remains are kept in a crypt below). The figures at the base are five women (the Five Days of the insurrection), a lion and an eagle (symbols of the courage and determination of the Milanese people).

1) Detail of the monument to the Five Days of Milan by G. Grandi.
2) The Rotonda della Besana, aerial view.

BASILICA OF S. MARIA DELLA PASSIONE

Founded at the end of the 15th century, it is the second largest church in Milan after the Duomo. The building work began around 1486 and only ended in 1729 when the façade was completed. In 1530 Cristoforo Lombardi finished the cupola with its octagonal tambour and in 1573 Martino Bassi designed the present three naves, altering the original Greek cross plan to a Latin cross. The baroque façade, begun in 1692, has four columns and is decorated with statues and reliefs, its low height enabling the splending octagonal lantern to be admired. The interior, dominated by the large octagonal cupola, is divided into three naves, the central one with the richly decorated vault (end of the 16th century), and the two side naves each with six chapels which house noteworthy 16th and 17th-century works of art. The most important ones are the many by Daniele Crespi *("Saints and Figures from the Lateran Order", "Ecce Homo" and "Scenes from the Passion", other*

"Scenes from the Passion", on the doors of the 17th-century organ on the left in the presbytery, *"Fasting of St. Charles"*). Also of considerable value are *"Deposition with St. Ambrose and St. Augustine"* by Bernardino Luini (1510-1515), *"The Last Supper"* by G. Ferrari (1543), the *"Crucifixion"* by G. Campi (1560), the 16th-century frescoes by Bergognone, A. Campi and Urbini and the 17th-century ones by C.F. Nuvolone, and the onyx medallions of the precious main altar painted by Procaccini and Cerano.

1-2) Two views of the interior of S. Maria della Passione.
3) The façade of the church.

1) The façade of the basilica of S. Carlo al Corso.
2) The façade of the church of S. Babila.
3) Via Bagutta, near the church of S. Babila, during one of the painting exhibitions held every year in spring and autumn, a recognised Milanese cultural event.

BASILICA OF S. CARLO AL CORSO

This majestic neoclassical church, begun by the architect Carlo Amati in 1838 and completed in 1847, stands in a piazza off Corso Vittorio Emanuele II, near Piazza San Babila. The site was previously occupied by the church of S. Maria dei Servi (from the old name of Corso Vittorio Emanuele: Corsia dei Servi) which was demolished in the 19th century to allow the Corso to be widened. A reminder of this former church is the statue of the Madonna in the Addolorata chapel of the present building. The church, flanked by two buildings perpendicular to it from whose base rises the Corinthian portico which extends into the pronaos of the church, has a triangular typanum on its façade. The exterior is dominated by the giant cupola and tambour decorated with Corinthian capital columns and alternating deep, empty niches and architraved windows. The interior has a spacious circular area, decorated in the lower order by Corinthian columns and chapels, and in the upper one by niches with statues of the saints framed by pilaster strips. Worthy of note is the vault in the presbytery, frescoed in 1864 by Angelo Inganni with *"Apotheosis of St. Charles" and "Figures of the Evangelists"* in the pendentives.

BASILICA OF SAN BABILA

The church of S. Babila stands at the corner between Corso Monforte and Corso Venezia, probably on the site of a 5th-century church founded by S. Lorenzo "ad *Concilia Sanctorum*". The original layout, or rather what remains of it (the building was in fact very controversially renovated between the 19th and 20th centuries, depriving it almost totally of its original appearance), possibly dates back to the 11th century. Between 1575 and the first decade of the 17th century the church was enlarged and a grandiose façade built, while between 1853 and 1926 total rebuilding was carried out which also included the rebuilding in the "Romanesque" style of a new façade and campanile. As a result of this work only the sides with windows, the main apse, the octagonal lantern and some capitals of the clustered pillars which define the three interior naves remain of the original church. The latter, with arches and a central barrel-vaulted nave, has 20th-century marble and mosaic decorations. At the side of the church, on the right-hand side of the courtyard, stands the so-called "Lion" column, built by Giuseppe Robecco in 1626 and which possibly depicts the ensign of the ancient city district of the eastern gate.

PALAZZO SERBELLONI

The impressive neoclassical building, built by Simone Cantoni in 1793 for the Serbelloni dukes, stands at the corner between Corso Venezia and Via S. Damiano. It is the result of extension of a 17th century palazzo of which the original front part facing towards Via S. Damiano still remains. Cantoni was responsible for the long, austere façade on Corso Venezia: with the architraved windows at the piano nobile, it has a large, central and recessed loggia, with huge Ionic columns and enormous double Ionic pillars, which define the elegant balustraded parapet. Partially hidden by the columns, a bas-relief of "*Episodes of the Lombard League*" runs along the wall of the loggia. The plain triangular tympanum at the top of the building has a large central window. The elaborate rectangular porch with its decorated barrel vault leads, through a series of porticos, to the inner garden and porticoed courtyard. The palazzo, seriously damaged by bombing in 1943 (which caused the loss of the sumptuous ballroom, the grand staircase and a valuable library) and later restored, represents a typical example of the architectural change which occurred in this area of the city at the turn of the 18th century. Having retained a somewhat modest appearance up until then, Corso Venezia (at that time Corsa di Porta Orientale), even after confiscation of religious property by the Austrian government from the numerous convents which stood there, was enlivened by building schemes which not only produced several palazzos, but also parks and gardens (such as the public gardens in the nearby Via Palestro, 1784) which in this period took on an importance almost equal to that of the buildings. This enthusiasm, which lasted into the 19th century, gave the area around Corso Venezia the elegant and aristocratic appearance which still distinguishes it today.

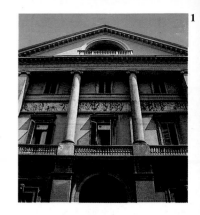

1) Detail of the façade.
2) Internal porch.
3) Façade of the palazzo.

1) Monument to Rosmini, by Confalonieri, in the Public Gardens.
2) The inner façade of the Villa
Reale.

VILLA REALE

An elaborate example of neoclassical villas, Villa Reale stands in Via Palestro. Piermarini was commissioned by Count Lodovico Barbiano di Belgioioso to design it, but he however entrusted the work to his pupil, Leopold Pollack, and only designed the interiors. The arrangement of the building is unusual for Milanese architecture, with the main façade facing inwards and the courtyard towards the street. The latter, in front of which stands a wall, seriously damaged by a bomb explosion in July 1993, has a central three-storey wing with four enormous Ionic columns, flanked by two side wings with two porticoed storeys. The rear side facing the English garden is much more attractive, formed by five wings of which the two end ones, with a triangular tympanum, and the central one, jut out, the former to a considerable extent, the latter only slightly. The façade is decorated with Ionic columns and pillars resting on the high rustic plinth of the ground floor and, between the windows of the two upper floors and in the two pediments, with mythological reliefs inspired by Parini. At the top the building has an elegant balustrade with statues of Greek and Roman gods. The refined neoclassical interiors (including a splendid room with a stuccoed vault in which marriages are performed) are almost all occupied by the Modern Art Gallery. Opposite the villa along Via Palestro are the Public Gardens (1783-1786) where, amongst waterfalls, ponds, false rocks and hills, stand ten monuments dedicated to famous Milanese figures of the 19th century.

MODERN ART GALLERY - PAVILION OF CONTEMPORARY ART

This gallery, whose basic, central collection consists of 19th-century works of art, particularly Lombard artists, is one of the richest in Italy. Its original collection, which included paintings, sculpture and graphic works for a total of around one thousand items, was dominated by mainly classical and academic taste, partly the result of the strong influence on Milanese artistic circles exerted by the Brera Academy and partly by the personal preferences of private collectors who donated their collections to the Gallery. Originally the Gallery was housed in some rooms of the Sforzesco Castle, which were nevertheless soon found to be inadequate for the increasing number of works, mostly coming from generous public donations. The problem of space, necessarily put aside when the first world war broke out, a period in which the Gallery, together with other Milanese museums and art galleries, was closed (as from 1915), resurfaced with its full gravity and urgency with the partial reopening of the Gallery in 1919. Finally, two years later, a large part of the collection (excluding the sculptures, drawings and graphic works, once again for reasons of space) was transferred to Villa Reale, which became the new location for the Gallery. The Villa, originally owned by Count Belgioioso, was purchased at the start of the 19th century by the French government and became the residence of Napoleon and his wife Josephine. From 1815, now with the name of Villa Reale, being owned by the royal family, it was used as the summer residence of the Viceroy of Italy, Eugenio di Beauharnais. It then fell into the hands of the Austrians and was occupied from 1857 until his death (the following year) by Radetzky. The Crown of Italy, who had owned it since the unification of Italy, finally gave it to the Commune of Milan in 1921. In the years leading up to the 1930's the collection continued to increase (thanks in part to purchases made in the fascist era and, mainly, to the many donations, including the extremely important one made in 1934 by A. Canavese who donated works by Boccioni, and that of E. Hoepli) and prolonged, or rather heightened, the problems of space. A merely partial solution to the problem included restoring some rooms of the Villa, enriching them with neoclassical furnishings, in which to

1) "Portrait of A. Manzoni" by F. Hayez.
2) "States of Mind, those going" by U. Boccioni.

house the sculptures left at the Sforzesco Castle. Further plans for solving the "space problem" were once again interrupted by the second world war and the gallery was closed to reopen later to the public in 1949. The damage suffered during the war required restoration work which coincided with the decision to construct a building to house the contemporary art collection. The building area chosen was that at the side of the Villa where the stables and stores once stood. The design was assigned to the architect Ignazio Gardella. The period between 1949 and 1954 saw the first Italian building commissioned and designed especially as regards layout and architecture to house contemporary works of art: the Padiglione d'Arte Contemporanea (Pavilion of Contemporary Art) known by the Milanese as the PAC. The structure, never really fully accepted by the critics due to the contrast (which some judge to be blatant) between its style and that of the Villa Reale, was seriou-

MODERN ART GALLERY - MAIN WORKS

In its splendid neoclassical rooms, the Gallery presents its works partly chronologically and partly grouped together in prestigious collections (Vismara, Italian and foreign works of the 20th century; Grassi, interesting above all due to the Italian and foreign works from the 19th and 20th centuries; Marino Marini Museum, paintings and sculptures by the great Italian artist including the famous *"Personalities of the 20th Century"*: De Pisis, Campigli, Carrà, Mies van der Rohe, Arp, Chagall, Moore). The most famous works include: portraits by A. Appiani; paintings by G. Carnovali known as "Il Piccio" (*Holy Family*); bronze and wax figures by M. Rosso (*"The Golden Age", "Laughing Child", "Ecce Puer"*); D. Induno, *"School for Seamstresses"*; works by F. Faruffini and bronzes by G. Grandi; T. Cremona, *"High Life", "Motherly Love"*; D. Ranzoni, *"The Children of Prince Trubetzkoy", "Portrait of Countess Arrivabene"*; G. Favretto, *"Anatomy Lesson"*; A. Fontanesi, *"Views"*; paintings by F. Palizzi (*"Animals"*); G. De Nittis, *"Femme aux Pompons", "Place des Invalides", "Portrait of Sarah Bernhardt"*; F. Zandomeneghi, *"Reading"*; V. Cabianca *"Nuns by the Sea"*; G. Fattori, *"Carabinieri on Patrol", "Grand Manoeuvres"*; T. Signorini, *"Oxen at Pietramala", "Clouds at Sunset"*; G. Boldini, *"Paris Street", "Young American Woman"*; G. Previati, *"The Sun King", "Noontide"*; A. Morbelli, *"Final Days", "The Central Station"*; M. Bianchi, *"Return from the Fair", "Snow in Milan"*; G. Pellizza da Volpedo, *"Fourth State"*; G. Segantini, *"Dead Chamois", "Angel of Life"*; A. Spadini, *"Anna in White"*; E. Boudin, *"Washerwomen"*; A. Sisley, *"Wind and Sun"*; lithographs by Toulouse-Lautrec; E. Vuillard, *"Portrait of Mrs. Hessel"*; C. Corot, *"Gust of Wind"*; Gauguin, *"Landscape in Brittany"*; Manet, *"Mr. Armand on Horseback"*; P. Bonnard, *"Interior by Lamplight"*; Cézanne, *"The Thieves and the Donkey"*; U. Boccioni, *"Portrait of Mother", "Portrait of Mrs. Casanova"*; G. Balla, *"Car-State of Mind", "Wife in Garden", "Car in Motion"*; G. Morandi, *"Landscape", "Still Life"*; works by V. Guidi, F. De Pisis, F. Pirandello, O. Rosai, C. Cagli, R. Guttuso, F. Casorati, Picasso, Matisse, Dufy, Van Gogh.

sly damaged by the terrible explosion of the attack on 27 July 1993 and had to be demoli-shed. The local administration however decided, in spite of opinions to the contrary, to rebuild it exactly as it was before in order to reopen this important arts centre as soon as possible.

1) "Anna in White" by A. Spadini.
2) "Portrait of the Countess Emilia Sommariva Seillère" by C. Bois-fremont de Boulanger.
3) "Anatomy Lesson" by G. Favretto.
4) "Landscape" by G. Morandi.

4

PALAZZO CUSANI

Situated in Via Brera and currently the seat of the Military Command of the Army Corps of Milan, the palazzo was built in the 17th century for the marquises, the brothers Cusani. In 1719 it was altered by Giovanni Ruggeri who produced the present baroque façade on Via Brera, while Giuseppe Piermarini later designed the neoclassical one looking out onto the garden. The majestic main front, with Corinthian pilaster strips, has open windows at the ground floor with a curved typanum which frames an oculus and, flanked by elaborately decorated double pilaster strips, two majestic portals. Positioned by the latter at the upper floor are two windows with balconies decorated with a stone balustrade and ornamental wrought iron scrolls. Corinthian pilaster strips also appear on the Piermarini façade looking onto the garden, with elegantly decorated windows. A large staircase with a red marble balustrade leads to the interior, with rooms overlooking the street decorated in the baroque style and those overlooking the porticoed courtyard decorated in the neoclassical style (some furnishings come from Palazzo Reale). The large salons, which exhibit paintings of that period, include the remarkable ballroom, where a large fresco from 1740 can be admired.

BRERA ART GALLERY

This art gallery is housed in the palazzo of the same name, built between the end of the 16th century and 1774 on the area once occupied by a convent of the Humiliati of the 14th century. Owned by the Jesuits from 1512, the building was extended in 1591 by Martino Bassi and radically altered in the 17th century to Richino's design. In 1772 the Jesuit order was suppressed and the palazzo was taken over by the Austrian government who set up a Fine Arts Academy and a collection of paintings there. Finally in 1774 Piermarini completed the building by adding the majestic entrance portal. The Gallery is entered from the grand staircase leading up from the inner courtyard of the palazzo, both masterpieces by Richini, in the centre of which stands a bronze statue designed by Antonio Canova and depicting Napoleon as Mars the peacemaker with Victory in his hand.

Opened in 1803, the Gallery initially was filled with a number of works of art from churches which had been closed down or acquired by Beauharnais. Between 1808 and 1809 it was therefore necessary to extend it, annexing the nearby 14th-century church of S. Maria di Brera from which two large frescoes by Vincenzo Foppa were taken: "*Madonna and Child between St. John the Baptist and St. John the Evangelist*" and "*Martyrdom of St. Sebastian*". In 1809 the Gallery of Art was officially inaugurated: a number of works continued to be acquired from all over Italy and later exchanges with European galleries were enacted. The damage caused by bombing in 1943 required massive rebuilding between 1946 and 1950.

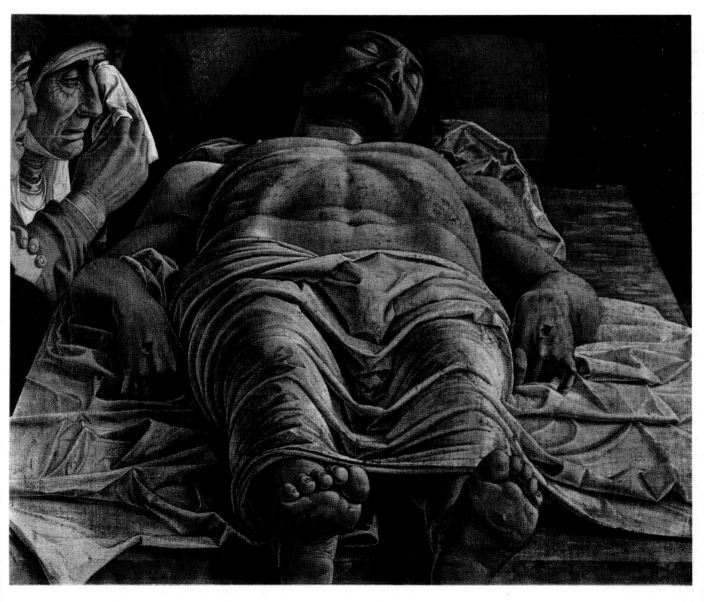

The masterpieces of the Gallery give a rough outline to the main sections: Venetian painting from the 15th to the 18th century, Lombard and Milanese painting, Emilian painting, Italian painting mainly by artists from central Italy of the 15th century, foreign painting, Italian painting of the 19th and 20th centuries. Since organisation of the rooms is subject to change, we have decided to provide here a brief overview of the main works in chronological order: Gentile da Fabriano, "*Coronation of the Virgin and Saints*" (polyptych of Valle Romita); Stefano da Zevio, "*Adoration of the Magi*"; B. Bembo, *"Tarot Cards"*; Mantegna, "*Dead Christ*", "*Madonna of the Cherubs*"; Francesco da Cossa, *"St. John the Baptist and St. Peter";* C. Crivelli, "*Madonna of the Candle*", "*Coronation of the Virgin*"; V. Foppa with the two frescoes mentioned above; B. Butinone, "*Madonna and Child and Saints Leonardo and Bernardino*"; Bergognone, "Madonna and Child and Holy Stefano Maconi"; Maestro della Pala Sforzesca, "*Madonna and Child*", "*The Doctors of the Church*", "*Lodovico il Moro and Beatrice d'Este*"; Piero della Francesca, "*Madonna and Child, Angels, Saints and Federico da Montefeltro*" (Pala di Montefeltro); Signorelli, "*Madonna of the Milk*", "*Flagellation*"; Raphael, *"Wedding of the Virgin*"; Bramante - frescoes from Palazzo Panigarola ("*Man of Arms", "The Cantor", "Man with Club", "Christ at the Column"*); A. de Predis, "Portrait of a Young Man"; A. Solari, *"Portrait of a Young Man"*; Bramantino, *"Madonna and Child and Offerer*", "Crucifixion"; Cesare da Sesto "*Madonna and Child";* Bernardino Luini, frescoes from the Villa della Pelucca near Monza and from the Chapel of S. Giuseppe of the Church of S. Maria della Pace; Marco d'Oggiono, "*The Archangels Defeating the Demon*"; G. B. Moroni, "*The Assumption";* Savoldo, "*Madonna*

1) **Inner courtyard of the Gallery of Art.**
2) **"The Kiss" by F. Hayez.**
3) **"The Supper at Emmaus" by Caravaggio.**

1) "The Temptation of St. Antonio" by G. Tiepolo.
2) "The Wedding of the Virgin Mary" by Raphael.

in *Glory and Saints"*; Moretto, *"The Assumption between St. Paul, St. Jerome, St. Catherine of Alexandria and St. Clare", "Madonna and Saints";* Giovanni Bellini, *"Madonna and Child"*; L. Lotto, *"Pietà"*; Carpaccio, *"Wedding of the Virgin", "Pietà", "The Discussion of St. Stephen";* Correggio *"Nativity"*; Veronese *"Supper at the House of the Pharisee", "Oration in the Garden"*; Tintoretto, *"Refinding of the Body of St. Mark"*; Annibale Carracci, *"The Samaritan at the Well"*; Agostino Carracci, *"The Adulterous Woman";* Guido Reni, *"Saints Peter and Paul"*; Guercino, *"The Renunciation of Agar"*; Caravaggio, *"Supper at Emmaus"*; Rubens, *"The Last Supper";* Tiepolo, *"The Temptation of St. Anthony"*; Canaletto, *"Views of the Canal Grande"*; Modigliani, *"Portrait of Kisling"*; Boccioni, *"The Brawl in the Galleria",* sketch for *"The City Rising"*; Carrà, *"The Metaphysical Muse"*; Severini, *"North-South"*; Sironi, *"Urban Landscape with Lorry"*; Arturo Martini, *"The Drinker"*; De Pisis, *"The Embankments of the Seine des Invalides", "San Moisé"*; Scipione *"Cardinal Vannuttelli on his Deathbed".*

1

2

FOURTH PART

THE SFORZESCO CASTLE

Between 1358 and 1368 Galeazzo II Visconti had a fortress built with the name of *"Castello di Porta Giovia"* after the nearby city gate. His successors began to live there in 1412 and extended it, maintaining its defensive purpose. Devastated and sacked after the death of Filippo Maria (1447), the castle was rebuilt by Francesco Sforza, who in 1452 entrusted the works to Filarete (who among other things built the famous clock tower). Ducal residence from 1466, throughout the 15th century it was enriched and embellished to become one of the most refined courts of that time, thanks also to the work of artists such as Vincenzo Foppa, Leonardo and Bernardino Zenale who decorated the interiors. Falling into the hands of the Spanish in the 16th century, it was converted into a highly efficient citadel with the building of the impressive ramparts laid out in a star in 1552 and the completion of the moats in the early 17th century. Partially destroyed by the French, it maintained its function as barracks until 1893, when Luca Beltrami began restoration work. Further restoration was carried out after the second world war.

1) **Entrance gate to the courtyard of the Rocchetta.**
2) **Detail of the Piazza d'Armi inside the Castello.**
3) **The coat of arms of the Viscontis.**
4) **An evocative view by night of the Castello with the tower by Filarete.**

The buildings, with a square base with 200 m sides, are surrounded by a dry moat. The main façade, with two cylindrical angular keeps (the two rear ones are square), has in the centre the entrance portal with the high tower by Filarete (rebuilt in 1905 by Beltrami). The other three sides, decorated like the façade with a crenellated screen and by windows with two lights reconstructed in the 19th century, have the same number of gates. The interior is divided into three parts: the spacious Piazza d'Armi, reached from the main entrance and corresponding to the original nucleus of the castle; the Rocchetta (on the left), formed by a group of buildings facing a splendid porticoed courtyard (the work of Filarete, Bramante and Ferrini) in which the Sforzas took refuge at the times of greatest danger, and the Ducal Court designed by Filarete (on the right) which housed the private apartments and the ducal reception rooms.

1) "The Young Woman Spinning" by G. Ceruti, known as Il Pitocchetto.
2) "Spring" by J. Bassano (detail).
3) "Madonna and Child" by V. Foppa.
4) "The Martyrdom of St. Sebastian" by V. Foppa.

1) Standard of the city depicting St. Ambrose and episodes from his life by G. Meda, 1565.
2) "The Rondanini Pietà" by Michelangelo.

MUSEUMS OF THE SFORZESCO CASTLE

The museums comprise the sections of the Civic Collections of Ancient and Applied Art and the two basement archaeological museums. The sculpture collection contains works from the 4th to the 16th centuries such as *"The Head of the Empress Theodora"* (6th century) and *"The Sepulchral Monument to Bernabò Visconti"* (14th century). One room houses the standard of the city (1566) in embroidered fabric. The Sala delle Asse has on its vault a complicated fresco of plants painted in 1497 by Leonardo da Vinci; 15th-century frescoes also decorate the ducal chapel. The Civic Collection of Arms (breastplates, swords and fire arms) contains the *"Portale del Banco Mediceo"* in marble, attributed to Michelozzo. The final room of the collection, the Scarlioni room, houses the *"Recumbent Statue of Gastone de Foix"* by Bambaia and the extremely well-known *"Rondanini Pietà"*, the last unfinished work by Michelangelo (1564). The Furniture Collection contains furnishings dating from the 15th to the 18th centuries and frescoes from the 15th century. The Civic Gallery of Art has 15th-century Italian works (Sano di Pietro, Filippo Lippi, Giovanni Bellini, Crivelli, Mantegna, Bembo), Lombard works of the 15th to 16th centuries (Bramantino, Bergognone, Cesare da Sesto, Correggio, Foppa, Moretto), portraits from the 15th to the 18th centuries (Lotto, Tintoretto, Titian, Van Dyck, Ceruti) and paintings by the leading baroque artists. This is followed by the Civic Collection of Applied Arts (ceramics and porcelain, clocks, costumes, scientific instruments), the Museum of Musical Instruments (including valuable Stradivarius and Guarneri violins). Hanging in the Ballroom (once used for receptions by the Sforzas), are the twelve *"Trivulzio tapestries"* or *"Tapestries of the Months"*, woven in early 1500 to cartoons by Bramantino.

ARCO DELLA PACE

Situated at the beginning of Corso Sempione, this impressive arch, one of the finest neo-classical monuments in Milan, was started in 1807 by Luigi Cagnola. The architect, who also designed the two customs houses at the sides, took his inspiration for the Arch, initially intended to celebrate Napoleon's victories and hence nicknamed Arco delle Vittorie, from the Roman Arches of Triumph with three barrel vaults. The works made slow progress, so much so that in 1815 the Austrians, returning to dominate the city, found it incomplete. It was the Emperor of Austria, in 1826, who intervened so that the work was completed, which was in any case only in 1838, five years after the death of its designer. Inaugurated in the presence of Ferdinand I, the arch was then named Arco della Pace in honour of peace in Europe in 1815. Made in Baveno granite and covered in Crevola marble, both faces have enormous fluted Corinthian columns resting on plinths decorated, like most of the surfaces, with allegorical bas-reliefs illustrating episodes of the fall of Napoleon (altered by Cagnola on the return of the Austrians). The faces also bear inscriptions, one dedicated to the entry into the city by Napoleon III and Victor Emmanuel II, the other to the independence of the Kingdom of Italy (originally there were epigraphs dedicated to Franz I and Ferdinand I of Austria), at whose sides stand statues depicting the Po and the Ticino rivers on one side, and the Adige and the Tagliamento on the other. On the attic at the top of the arch rests the bronze *"Coach-and-Six of Peace"* by A. Sangiorgio, with the four *"Victories on Horseback"* by G. Putti at the four corners.

1) **Il Palazzo dell'Arte**
2) **Arco della Pace by L. Cagnola at the beginning of Corso Sempione.**

PALAZZO DELL'ARTE

This modern structure, built between 1932 and 1933, stands in Viale Alemagna, surrounded by the Sempione Park. Designed by Giovanni Muzio, it was commissioned by Senator Antonio Bernocchi to house the Triennial Exhibition of Decorative Arts, begun in 1923 to allow constructive comparison between Italian and international manufacture. The main façade is enlivened by large light-coloured arches which stand out against the terracotta-covered background, while the front facing the park has an arcade, covered in pink marble like the arches. The interior, on three storeys and with spacious rooms, houses a majestic grand staircase.

BASILICA OF S. MARIA DELLE GRAZIE

Building of the basilica started in 1463 from a design by Guiniforte Solari and was radically altered as early as 1492 by Bramante, commissioned by Lodovico il Moro. The sloping façade, in masonry decorated with pointed-arch windows and oculi like the side, has a central marble portal with slim columns in front on which a round arch canopy rests. The basilica is closed off at the back by the impressive three-apse tribune with a sixteen-side lantern circled by architraved two-light windows and arches on double columns. The interior, with three naves, defined by ogival arches resting on columns and with entirely frescoed vaults, has decorated chapels on both sides with important frescoes and paintings, including that of "*S. Maria delle Grazie*", existing prior to the basilica to which it gives its name. The tribune and the presbytery are also richly decorated and lead to the fine cloisters designed by Bramante. The back wall of the refectory preserves the world-renowned "*Last Supper*" by Leonardo da Vinci.

1) **Exterior: the tribune by Bramante.**
2) **Overall view of the Basilica.**
2) **Interior: the central nave**
4) **The cloisters.**

Pages 72-73

1) **"The Last Supper" by Leonardo da Vinci.**
2-3-4-5) **Details.**

LEONARDO DA VINCI'S LAST SUPPER

Leonardo da Vinci worked on the "*Last Supper*" for approximately two years, between 1495 and 1498. Commissioned by Lodovico il Moro, the artist worked intermittently, nevertheless creating what is unanimously considered one of the masterpieces of Renaissance art. The room in which the Supper is set, lit by a transverse band of light aimed at the right wall, continues ideally that of the refectory, extended in perspective in the pictorial representation. The scene depicts the moment in which Christ, in the centre, announces to his disciples, in groups of three, that one of them will betray Him. Leonardo succeeded magnificently in showing the emotion aroused in each of them by the announcement by Jesus, whose face reveals a mixture of acceptance and deep sadness. The disciples, shown performing gestures typical of those seated at a table (drinking, blowing on the food, holding a knife in one hand etc.), show in their mannerisms and in the expressions on their faces incredulity and surprise, some looking towards the Lord, others remarking to each other about these grave utterings. Judas, fourth from the left, is turned towards Christ and clutches the bag containing the thirty pieces of silver. Leonardo did not use oils for the painting, but instead strong tempera on two layers of plaster. This new technique was not however very resistant to the humidity in the room, so much so that in 1518 the work was partly damaged and at the end of the century was considered virtually lost. Between the 18th century and the outbreak of the second world war (from which the painting emerged unscathed) numerous and not always successful restoration operations were carried out, which the works performed in the second half of our century have partially remedied in order to recover the work completely and to preserve it from possible causes of further damage.

1

4

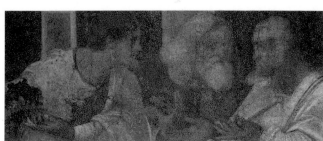

5

BASILICA OF S. AMBROGIO

This great church, with a Romanesque four-sided portico in front which holds the remains of frescoes and marble sculptures, has an open sloping façade on two orders of arches (the five of the upper loggia arranged in decreasing order) flanked by two campaniles: the one by Monaci (on the right) from the 9th century and the one by Canonici from the 12th century. The interior, with three naves with cross-vaults resting on clustered pillars richly decorated in the capitals, octagonal lantern and raised presbytery ending in the semicircular apse, contains masterpieces of Romanesque art such as the pulpit recomposed in the 12th century, the Stilicone sarcophagus beneath it (4th century) with elaborate sculpture decorations, the canopied cyborium (10th century) which stands above the extremely valuable altar by Volvinio (835) covered in gold and silver leaf, and the priceless golden sacellum of S. Vittore in Ciel d'oro with frescoes by Tiepolo and a cupola entirely covered with 14th-century frescoes.

1) **Central part of the "Golden Altar" or "Altar-Facing".**
2) **The monuments of St. Ambrose.**
3) **The "Pusterla" (or smaller gate), the only remaining one of the medieval walls, with the statue of St. Ambrose between St. Gervaso and St. Protasio.**
4) **The façade of the Basilica.**

BRIEF HISTORY

It was founded in 379 by St. Ambrose (later buried there in 397) in an area near a Christian cemetery where small basilicas stood to house the holy relics of martyrs, including S. Vittore. The original church, with three naves defined by columns and with no transept, was identical in size to the present one, not including the chapels. It soon took on considerable importance, so much so that in the centuries which followed bishops were anointed and coronations held there. Towards the end of the 8th century a Benedictine monastery was built next to the basilica and the church underwent changes: the bowl-shaped vault of the apse was replaced by the presbytery and two small apses were added to the side naves. In the 9th century the Archbishop Ansperto commissioned the building of a large atrium in front of the church and the Monaci campanile was erected. The crypt was formed below the presbytery (where the urn with St. Ambrose's relics are kept) and Volvinio created in 835 the precious altar-facing or gold altar beneath the ciborium. Between the 10th and 12th centuries further work was performed on the crypt, the apses and the Ansperto atrium, and major work was carried out on the exterior with building of the Canonici campanile and the façade with sloping upper arches and the rebuilding of the lantern, the building of the large pillars to support the naves, the forming of women's galleries and the chapel of St. Bartholomew. In 1196 the third span of the central nave collapsed and new cross-vaults were required to replace the old wooden roofing. The following years were relatively quiet for the basilica, which was however later modified in the early 15th century when the small basilica of S. Vittore (dating from the 4th century) was connected to the church. In 1492 Lodovico il Moro commissioned Bramante to design the left presbytery, although the works were interrupted in 1499 when Lodovico fell from power. In 1572 Charles Borromeo called upon Pellegrini to redesign the lantern and at the end of the 16th century the chapels were completed. In the 18th century the consolidation works were begun, the crypt beneath the presbytery was rebuilt and Tiepolo worked in the church. From 1857 to the end of the 19th century major restoration and rebuilding work was carried out to return it to the characteristic appearance of the 12th century. Further work was necessary after the extensive damage caused by bombing in 1943.

MUSEUM OF SCIENCE AND TECHNOLOGY

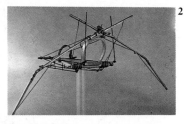

This museum is housed in the former convent of S. Vittore, rebuilt in the 16th century by the Olivetani monks on the foundations of an older Benedictine monastery. With its vast collection of instruments, machinery, drawings and documentation, it was opened in 1953 to celebrate the fifth centenary of the birth of Leonardo da Vinci, to whom an entire gallery was dedicated. The latter displays models and reproductions of his drawings for all the technical and scientific branches investigated by the great artist, each one accompanied by thorough explanations. The museum comprises various sections in which, through models, original instruments and machinery and information boards, the history is told from the start up to the latest advances of industry and the textiles, metallurgy, car manufacture, naval, aeronautical, agricultural, transport, goldsmithery, coinage, graphics, cinema and photography, timekeeping, acoustics, optics, astronomy, modern physics and computer technologies.

BASILICA OF S. MAURIZIO AL MONASTERO MAGGIORE

Begun in 1503 and attributed to Dolcebuono, this church was part of the ancient Benedictine convent demolished in the second half of the 19th century. It has a plain façade with three levels, whose decoration continues up to the left side, at the end of which stands the square bell tower (the lower part consists of remains of the Roman circus which occupied the site). The fine interior has a single nave divided into two areas (the first for the congregation, the second reserved at one time for the nuns) and is covered by a vault with lunettes, with chapels at the sides. The whole surface is covered in splendid frescoes, mostly by Bernardino Luini, his followers and other artists of the time (including Bramantino, Boltraffio, Peterzano and V. Foppa). Outstanding among the works by Luini are *"The Flagellation of Christ"*, *"The Martyrdom and Beheading of St. Catherine"* in the third chapel, *"The Martyrdom of St. Maurice"* and the cycle of *"The Passion of Christ"* on the dividing wall.

Museum of Science and Technology - Leonardo da Vinci.
1) Model of a flying machine.
2) Model of an "omitottero".
3) Model of an excavating machine.
4) Model of a revolving bridge.
5) The rococo façade of Palazzo Litta, added by Bolla in 1700 to the palazzo built by Richini and commissioned by Count Arese in 1648.
6) Interior of S. Maurizio al Monastero Maggiore with frescoes by B. Luini and other 16th-cent. painters of the Lombard school.
7) "The martyrdom of St. Catherine of Alessandria", fresco by B. Luini inside the Basilica, 1530.

MEAZZA STADIUM (FORMERLY S. SIRO)

The area of the stadium was occupied by a hippodrome from 1887 to 1925 when the industrialist Piero Pirelli had a football ground built with four rectilinear grandstands, partially under cover, and a capacity of approximately 35,000 spectators. Bought by the city council in 1935, the ground was altered in the same year (adding four curves to link up the stands and enlarging the two main ones for a total capacity of 50,000) and in 1954 (building of a second grandstand tier, partly covering existing ones with access via spiral ramps and stairs for a theoretical capacity of 100,000, reduced to 80,000 for safety reasons). In 1990, for the

World Cup, the stadium, dedicated in 1980 to the footballer, Giuseppe Meazza, was further refurbished, with designs by Giancarlo Regazzi and Enrico Hoffer, adding a third tier of seats for a total capacity of 86,000 persons. The structure of these stands rests on eleven cylindrical reinforced concrete towers, four of which extend beyond the stands to support the mesh roofing which leaves only the pitch uncovered. The towers contain the access routes to the stands.

PIAZZA DELLA REPUBBLICA

An extremely busy road junction, until the 1930's this piazza was the location for the old central railway station, built between 1857 and 1864, for trains connecting Milan to the main Italian cities and European capitals. The increase in rail traffic and building development led in 1931 to the demolition of this station, replaced the same year by today's Central Station in Piazza Duca d'Aosta. A number of buildings look onto the Piazza, including four skyscrapers at the corners, built between 1940 and 1960.

1) Outside view of the Stadium.
2) The interior of the Stadium, seen from the third tier at the inauguration of the 1990 World Cup.

CENTRAL STATION AND PIRELLI SKYSCRAPER

Dominating the Piazzale Duca d'Aosta, this immense station was built in the early 1930's as the central junction for almost all Milan's rail traffic. Approved in 1912, the design by Ulisse Stacchini was not implemented until 1926 and then only completed in 1931. The Art Nouveau style building, later adapted to celebrate the fascist regime, is formed by a huge front part (207 m long) in stone and marble, with a central projecting part, sculpture groups on top and three monumental entrances, flanked by two smaller wings also with three entrances. Inside is a gallery, heavily decorated with allegorical medallions, which leads to the large ticket hall, also decorated with reliefs and statues. From this hall two marble staircases and two escalators lead to the front gallery, whose internal wall is decorated with enormous ceramic panels depicting views of Milan and the main Italian cities. The tracks, flanked by platforms, are covered by giant rooves in iron and glass, supported by robust piers.

On the left side in front of the station stands the spectacular Pirelli skyscraper, built between 1955 and 1959. It is the tallest building in Milan (127 m) and, when it was built, was also the first to exceed the total height of the Duomo. It stands on the site of the first Pirelli factory and was the administrative headquarters of the company until the end of the 1970's, when, maintaining the nickname of "Pirellone", it was sold to the Lombardy Region.

1) **Piazza della Repubblica.**
2) **The Central Station and, on the left, the Pirelli skyscraper.**

ABBEY OF CHIARAVALLE

Founded by Bernardo di Clairvaux and built between the second half of 1100 and 1221 and later extended up to the 18th century, it is undoubtedly the most important monument just outside Milan. It has valuable architectural features, including the fine 14th century tower-lantern and the cloisters designed by Bramante (rebuilt after destruction by the French in 1861), and works of art, including delicate frescoes (some from the 14th century, but mostly by Flemish artists) and the splendid carved wooden choir-stalls from the 17th century.